T0374228

THE MYSTERY OF GOD

Hidden Truths since Timeless Times

CLINTON CRUICKSHANK

Copyright © 2022 Clinton Cruickshank.

All rights reserved. No part of this book may be used or reproduced by any means, graphic, electronic, or mechanical, including photocopying, recording, taping or by any information storage retrieval system without the written permission of the author except in the case of brief quotations embodied in critical articles and reviews.

WestBow Press books may be ordered through booksellers or by contacting:

WestBow Press
A Division of Thomas Nelson & Zondervan
1663 Liberty Drive
Bloomington, IN 47403
www.westbowpress.com
844-714-3454

Because of the dynamic nature of the Internet, any web addresses or links contained in this book may have changed since publication and may no longer be valid. The views expressed in this work are solely those of the author and do not necessarily reflect the views of the publisher, and the publisher hereby disclaims any responsibility for them.

Any people depicted in stock imagery provided by Getty Images are models, and such images are being used for illustrative purposes only. Certain stock imagery © Getty Images.

Scriptures taken from the Holy Bible, New International Version®, NIV®. Copyright © 1973, 1978, 1984, 2011 by Biblica, Inc.™ Used by permission of Zondervan. All rights reserved worldwide. www.zondervan.com The "NIV" and "New International Version" are trademarks registered in the United States Patent and Trademark Office by Biblica, Inc.®

ISBN: 978-1-6642-7289-7 (sc)
ISBN: 978-1-6642-7290-3 (hc)
ISBN: 978-1-6642-7288-0 (e)

Library of Congress Control Number: 2022913174

Print information available on the last page.

WestBow Press rev. date: 8/2/2022

Praise for *The Mystery of God: Hidden Truths since Timeless Times*

This book marked a watershed moment in my life. It offers a clear, simple, summarized interpretation of God's purposes for humankind. I feel that the author was enlightened by great wisdom and authority to bring us this valuable material.

Ricardo Adolfo Lineros, systems engineer, Republic of Venezuela

This wonderful book, full of great truths and astonishing lessons, unquestionably reflects God's character, His unconditional love for all of us, and His deep confidence in this writer, who was entrusted with the mission of setting it before us. It will be a source of blessing for everyone.

Dr. Ricardo McKenzie, MD, Laguna Niguel, California, USA

This book is an easy, enjoyable read. It covers a full range of relevant topics for learning about the mystery of God. It reveals hidden spiritual truths and treasures that not only impart knowledge but also strengthen our faith. The exceptional content of this book is innovative, fun to read, and very useful.

Richard Gerli Hand, member and founder of the first Costa Rican chapter of the Full Gospel Business Men's Fellowship International (FGBMFI)

There can be no doubt that this book unveils the mystery of God to give us a clear perspective on our many questions about why God does what He does. It also leads us into deep introspection about who we are compared to the grandeur of God, His immense love, and His eternal purpose for every one of us. This is why all of us should read this excellent, revealing, hope-filled book.

Saray Amador, president of Telefides, the Costa Rican, Catholic television channel, and the Costa Rican Chamber of Radio and Television

This book demonstrates that there is great blessing in knowing, loving, and serving God. The greatest mystery that was kept hidden but revealed, according to Colossians 1:27, is, "Christ in you, the hope of glory." Moreover, glory is the physical, visible expression of the invisible, spiritual character of God.

Marco Pérez, founder of the first Costa Rican chapter of the Full Gospel Business Men's Fellowship International (FGBMFI) and Portantorchas Biblical School

The Mystery of God distills the ecumenical foundation of the Old and New Testaments and the spiritual and pragmatic elements of the Judeo-Christian tradition, providing the basis and guidelines for a more comprehensive understanding of God's purpose in creating the universe and especially humankind.

Mike Gucovsky, a former deputy undersecretary at the UN for Latin America and the Caribbean

As I read this book, I was filled with a growing sense of wonder at the tremendous effort the author has made to write down and share truths hidden from time eternal. I could do nothing less than sit down, read it again, and try to internalize these truths. The book motivated me to rethink the transcendental topics developed in each chapter, and I will continue to read it over, little by little, in the coming months, to meditate on its content and fully internalize it.

Teófilo de la Torre, three-time executive president of the Costa Rican Institute of Electricity and minister of environment and energy of Costa Rica

CONTENTS

PREFACE

Nowadays, many people, including believers, find their hearts awash with great confusion and disappointment. Materialistic, humanistic philosophy has invaded the world, wreaking havoc in human hearts and lives and causing many to lose their fear of God. All this distances them from their Creator, worsens their confusion and frustration, and feeds the despair that grows in the shadows of doubt, skepticism, and ignorance.

This book will provide eye-opening answers to over three-dozen weighty questions, many of which have intrigued generations of thinkers and scholars from time immemorial. The Lord has given us surprising glimpses and tantalizing tastes of a divine view, which gives us a peek into His mystery—*the mystery of God.*

These glimpses bring the need to create new terms and use a variety of similes, as a way to explain spiritual matters, which until now, have stood as troubling riddles to the human mind. The similes you will find here take the shapes of new terms and new ideas, including the *Hologram Principle* and the *Inverse Hologram Principle.*

Both provide a means of explaining, for example, the mystery of the holy Trinity of God.

There will be other new words as well, such as *co-inherency* and *triple co-inherency* (*Trinitarian co-inherency)*, that will be used to explain the mutual indwelling of the Spirit of God and the human soul and the dwelling among the three persons of the Trinity of God. Other new terms are *primary receiving channel (PRC)*, which portrays the exclusive medium that God uses to communicate with us, and *secondary receiving channel (SRC),* which is the way that other spiritual beings communicate with human beings. Another is *infinite infrastructure*, which explains the divine throne that allows the Spirit of God to coexist with and in the human soul. There are many more.

You will also see how human unbelief can lead to ignoring your declared enemy, the devil, whose purpose it is to undermine your faith, distance you from God, and finally, take control of your soul. You will see that he goes to any length to fulfill his purpose. He even takes God's truths, distorts them (demonizes them), and tries to take them for himself so that he can deceive people and turn them away from God's path.

At such a time as this, *The Mystery of God* has been revealed to reaffirm to believers that God himself, the Almighty, dwells inside us so that we can place our full trust in Him to wipe all fear, confusion, and despair from our hearts and anchor our souls in that hope. As with Abraham, we will learn to hope against all hope. Even when hope seems to have vanished, we will not let go.

This book will clear up the apparent paradox or contradiction that God cannot be contained by anything in the universe or even the universe itself. At the same time, He is contained in the hearts of millions of men and women all over the world. He dwells within them through His Holy Spirit. This is possible because of the infinite infrastructure that Almighty God created in the human beings. The divine throne in the human heart is a type of coupling station, which allows God to coexist with people.

The Mystery of God also reveals how the Lord, who is the one and only one, performed the miracle so that the fullness of God would always and simultaneously be present in the three persons of the divine Trinity. At the same time, He is present in the hearts of millions and millions of believers, without ever losing his wholeness. After all, God is still one and the same. Another surprising and unequaled but understandable fact is that God's children (the believers) are the shared spiritual essence of God (their father) and the bride of the Lamb (their mother), just as human children are the shared carnal essence of their earthly mother and father.

The Lord will surprise us when He reveals what the New Jerusalem really is. From time immemorial, the heart has been God's dwelling place. In the beginning, He dwelt in His own heart. Later, He dwelt in the hearts of His believing sons and daughters and also, in the bride of the Lamb, which as we will see is the New Jerusalem—neither more nor less than the very heart of God. This confirms that God always lives in hearts.

We are powerfully moved by the dramatic, spectacular conversion of Jacob on his travels to the home of his uncle Laban in Paddan Aram. His conversion leaves us with extraordinary teachings regarding the strictly personal and particular nature of the relationship between God and each one of us as human beings.

God teaches us the reason why He is the Alpha and the Omega. He clears up the difference between himself as God the Alpha and himself as God the Omega while remaining the one and only God.

Thus, He leads us into the true mystery that is, embodied in the endless blood sacrifices of animals. He shows us that from the fall of Adam and Eve until the death and resurrection of Jesus Christ, these sacrifices allowed the Lord to replace one life with another. Thus, they kept His human children alive despite their never-ending sins and transgressions.

This summary is but an introduction or a sampling to whet your appetite to the extraordinary revelations that you will find in this book. They do not cease to astonish and reaffirm that we stand before a singular, unique, awesome, indescribable, and uncontainable God, to use only a few of the many descriptors that will always fall short of portraying who He is.

Clinton Cruickshank

ACKNOWLEDGMENTS

I would like to take this opportunity to honor and recognize the following people.

To Almighty God, my Father, who entrusted these revelations and hidden truths to this frail, defective vessel. To Him be the glory, honor, and all recognition as the spiritual author and inspiration of this book.

To my wife, Ingrid, my better half, who lovingly counseled me, encouraged me, and stood by my side for the many hours that I sat before my Bible and stared at my computer, during the process of writing this text.

To my son Clinton Jr., whose knowledge and discernment of God's will, are awe-inspiring and whom the Lord used to bless and support me beyond my expectations, with his keen, accurate comments, which significantly improved the process.

To my daughter, Angie whose sensitivity to God's voice and the familiarity with which He treats her was of great support in the most difficult moments to reaffirm my trust in the immense mercy and grace of our Lord Jesus Christ.

To Pastoress Sofia Quintanilla, who, with her ever-present loving-kindness, agreed to perform the first in-depth review of the manuscript of this book.

While I never had the blessing of meeting him, to deceased televangelist Harvey Ben Kinchlow (Ben Kinchlow), who, through his years of obedience to God and his devotion to *The 700 Club*, allowed God to use him as a mighty instrument to lead many lost souls to the throne of divine grace. I am deeply honored to be part of this group of men and women.

INTRODUCTION

A Cautionary Note for Readers

You will derive more benefit as you read this book if you make an effort to set aside your own ideas and do not hurry to reject or dismiss the information that you will find here. You need to let go of all your preconceived notions. If you do not like what you are reading, take a moment to ask the Lord whether these words are His. Ask Him for wisdom, discernment, and an understanding heart so that you can assimilate this message fully.

In view of the number and quality of revelations contained herein, a second or third reading of some paragraphs, chapters, or even the whole book could be useful to help you clarify and better process every truth that you will find here. It will predispose your heart to the purposes that the Lord is revealing in His mystery.

Finally, if you disagree with any of the ideas here, you would do well not to dismiss them out of hand or stop reading the rest of the book. You might miss out, on receiving the blessings in the rest of it.

Chapter 1

GOD'S REVELATIONS

For several years now, I have made it a practice to read the Bible daily. This discipline brings me closer to God and improves my understanding of His Word, character, and purposes. I have come to experience less failure, wrongheadedness, and rebellion in my life, all of which were far too frequent. But Bible reading helped shape my character and improve my relationships. More particularly, it is the best support available for building and sustaining my faith, curtailing my pride and arrogance, and thinking of others more than myself.

1.1. How the Revelations Began

Around mid-October 2007, I began to receive a series of revelations of unaccustomed clarity. Because of the content, I understood that these were revelations from God and began to write them down. I then checked them against the Bible and shortly thereafter, began to share some of them, first with my family and then with a few believing friends.

The revelations were building in intensity, frequency, and greater transcendence. They became so frequent and intense that I began to take notepaper with me at all times so that I could write them down quickly. The words often came with such urgency that I had to rummage around for scraps of paper from the family desk. My wife, Ingrid, suggested that I buy a small notebook. They would even come when I was in the middle of a shower. This required me special efforts to be able to register them opportunely.

1.2. But Why Me?

For the years that I have been in the faith, in active militancy and commitment to the Lord Jesus Christ, I can affirm that I am a believer with some degree of maturity and that I have and maintain an important relationship with Him. I also recognize and confess that I am not as perfect in God's eyes as I am called to be nor as obedient as I ought to be. As I became more aware of the depth and significance of these revelations, I began to wonder, *Why me? Who am I that the Lord would trust me with such material?*

I asked myself these questions time after time. I confess that I did not dare to ask the Lord directly. I was reluctant to muddy the waters and run even the slightest risk of contradicting Him. I did not want to end up losing the anointing or extinguishing the astonishing revelations I had been receiving. At least, it was what I thought at the time. Even so, the question did not stem from mere foolishness or vanity. But I wanted to know what I had been doing right for God to show me such special grace. I wanted to know what it was so that I could keep doing it even more.

I also got to thinking about the way that I was living and the things that had become important in recent years. As I considered all this, I was able to identify certain facts and features. They might explain why the Lord, in His measureless mercy and grace, had noticed that I was a servant whom He could reveal and entrust with these truths. He even provided instructions to make them known to all people—especially His own. I want to examine some of these facts. I hope that they can shed light on and answer the daunting question of why me?

1.2.1. Psalms 51:10

> Create in me a pure heart, O God, and renew a steadfast spirit within me. (Psalms 51:10).

My mother, Mrs. Pearl, is now with the Lord. She was the first one who drew my attention to the importance of Psalms 51, especially this verse. She was a woman who lived a simple, happy life. God blessed her abundantly with eight children.

All of them believers. She was poor in material resources, but she seemed to always have enough. Indeed, she was one of those people through whom Jesus Christ often replicated the miracle of multiplying the loaves and fish. Mrs. Pearl somehow always managed to feed everyone with very little. This included her family, their friends, schoolmates, and university classmates, neighbors, and many others. There was always something left over. God also blessed her with the skill to turn out splendid, delicious meals.

She suffered from a chronic illness for many years. Her heart was always filled with joy, even though she lived her last twenty-five years with only one leg, as the result of amputation. My mother always radiated joy. She was able to extend encouragement to everyone else. She was the hub that the entire family revolved around. While she never interfered, she somehow helped couples work out their spats. She was a wonderful family counselor, exceedingly generous, and always ready to offer the only thing she had to share: something to eat. Mrs. Pearl had a clean heart, she was pure and kind, and a righteous spirit guided all her actions.

I thank God for allowing me to honor her. I often went to see her. I remember a loving conversation that occurred during one of my visits. I asked where her strength and purity of heart came from. It always shone from her peaceful face, her great compassion, and the hymns and worship songs that she hummed all day long as she cooked, ironed, cleaned, and went about her domestic chores. She told me that she always leaned on Psalms 51, especially verse 10. She quoted it in English, the language of her childhood. She said that every day, she renewed her petition for God to give her a pure heart and a steadfast spirit before Him.

Psalms 51 became one of my favorite Psalms. For years, I followed Mrs. Pearl's example. I put this Bible verse before me as I cried out for God to purify my heart. I know that God has had mercy on me. He keeps my heart pure, despite my many weaknesses, faults, and rebellions.

1.2.2. My Introductory Prayer before Reading the Bible

My life underwent a major transition in 1994. I found myself sliding into sadness and depression. I did not know it at the time, but it was the Lord leading me to a crossroads. I would need to wake up and set aside the self-sufficiency, pride, and arrogance that had marked my life until then.

Thanks to my parents, I had always believed in God. But because of my foolishness, lack of humility, and excessive self-reliance, I had never fully surrendered to Him. I was deep in my arrogance, pride, ignorance, and foolishness. I had always thought that people who went into depression were weak, and above all, they had no character. I never thought I could become depressed. In 1994, I began to show symptoms of sadness and depression. I spun into a state of helplessness. I was filled with anxiety and fear, even to the point of being afraid to leave my house. I lived through this drama for nearly two weeks.

Then one Saturday morning in June, I was at home, alone, sad, anxious, and distressed. I did not know how to shake off such a terrible sensation. I turned on the television to relieve my anxiety. I was immediately drawn to *The 700 Club.* That was where I saw Pastor Ben Kinchlow. I instantly sensed that Pastor Kinchlow was speaking directly to me. He said that it did not matter what problems I had. God was much bigger than any of them were. And, if I surrendered my life to the Lord Jesus Christ and invited Him into my heart, He would give me peace, despite all my problems and circumstances.

I had claimed for many years that someday I would accept Jesus Christ, but that I was still too young for such a thing. I was not yet ready to take on the boring life of a Christian. I was so blind and foolish. I had such poverty of knowledge and understanding!

Right then, however, I needed that peace, no matter how much it cost. The distress was making me feel utterly powerless. For the first time in my life, I sensed that I had lost all control. Even the floor seemed unsteady beneath my feet. I was not accustomed to such things. To be honest, the sensation was awful. This was how I ended up accepting

Pastor Kinchlow's invitation to receive Jesus Christ into my heart. I would do anything to just relieve the distress and anxiety that I was feeling.

As I finished the act of accepting and receiving Jesus Christ into my heart, they invited their viewers to call in, and I did exactly that. I followed every instruction like a soldier. I was desperate to shake off that terrible sense of despair. A sister in the faith answered my telephone call. Even today, I do not know who she was, but I continue asking God to bless her mightily. She was very friendly, and she explained that I should start reading the Bible at the Gospel of John. She said that before opening the book, I should first offer the following prayer and ask the Lord to guide me:

> Holy Spirit, help me to understand your Word, You who inspired it, give me the gift of revelation. **You be my teacher and my guide**.

All these years later, I still extend that petition to the Lord every time I sit down to read His Word.

1.2.3. Asking for the Lord's Wisdom and Revelation

Also, I have been asking the Lord for wisdom and revelation for a long time. I paraphrase Ephesians 1:17 like this:

> Glorious Father, give me the spirit of wisdom and revelation in the knowledge of God, his Word, his purposes and of His creation. I ask this in the mighty name of Jesus. Amen.

Now, please allow me the following digression. One of my favorite hobbies and greatest pleasures as a child was to gaze at the sky, especially on starry nights, and contemplate the stars and the immensity of the universe. In those days, the nighttime's landscape of the countryside was the perfect place to observe God's grandeur and His wondrous creation.

I must admit that today, even more than when I was a child, the Lord keeps me filled with awe and deeply moved by His grandeur, His majesty, and the immensity of His creation. I live in constant wonder, for everything about God is so stunning, so infinite, if you will. This form of infinity deepens in every direction. It extends from infinitely small to infinitely large so that the small and the large converge in the infinite.

It is said that our galaxy holds billions of stars and that the universe holds billions of galaxies. All this serves to reveal more clearly the magnificence of the Creator and His entire creation. This wonder that God created keeps me in a permanent state of awe regarding who He is.

Here, I meekly confess that the Lord has not only heard my plea but has also granted my wish because He has truly enlightened my understanding and has placed in me a spirit of wisdom and revelation to know God, His Word, His purposes, and His creation. I say these things with the greatest humility and full respect for everyone who may read these words. I would rather risk looking foolish in the eyes of others than not honoring the Lord with the truth.

I still face the question of why me? The answer may lie in the explanation that I have just given: I asked the Lord with humility and submission to give me a pure heart—something I truly desired—to give me understanding of His Word, and to have a spirit of wisdom and revelation in the knowing God. This explanation is mine because in this, I have received no revelation, but I give my opinion.

1.3. And the Revelations Continue

Having taken that digression, I should now explain that the revelations continued with increasing intensity. In the midst of them, the Lord sowed His purposes in my heart that they should be compiled, preserved in a book, and to be known to the world and most of all, to His people. Then I wondered what the title of such book would be. I discussed it with Ingrid, and she suggested that I wait for the Lord to reveal His own title.

I continued to receive more and more revelations, which left me ever more astonished. Given that these revelations carried great knowledge, purposes, and truths, I began to find answers for many questions, which heretofore had been unknown.

I collected the scraps of paper, handwritten notes, and my notebook and began copying them into a computer file. It seemed that up to that point, they were not coming in any particular order. I could hardly imagine sorting through all that information and figuring out a clear connecting thread, which I was certain that it had. I also realized that the Lord was not going to just dump all these revelations into my lap and expect me to write a book on my own. Even so, I must confess that it all seemed a bit overwhelming. I was slow to begin the project.

Life brings moments when you simply cannot continue procrastinating, delaying a project, and taking no action, particularly if it is God's project. I sensed that the time had come, and I began to work on an outline of the procedures that I would follow and a list of topics based on my notes. It was a moving target because the revelations were still coming, albeit less intensely.

I finally began to write and flesh out each one of the themes. I admit that as I write these lines, about 30 percent of the book has now been developed, and I have yet to receive the Lord's revelation of a title. Even so, I write on and trust that He would give me the title at the right time. I eagerly await that moment.

God has spared nothing to make these revelations available to me. He has demonstrated His immense creativity and used a great variety of means to communicate them. Here are a few examples:

- ✓ Through direct communication to my heart
- ✓ Through His written Word
- ✓ Through sermons by pastors
- ✓ Through prophecies
- ✓ Through worship songs
- ✓ Through His majestic creation
- ✓ Through movies or films
- ✓ Through certain books
- ✓ Through the internet
- ✓ Through certain television programs and more

I often find that while I am listening to a sermon on some particular point of scripture, the Lord uses the message to reveal something utterly different from the specific points being elucidated, or explained in the pastor's words. He fits it all together. There is no discrepancy between the sermon and the revelations. It is amazing!

The method the Lord used with the greatest frequency and intensity was revelations directly communicated to my heart, which was how I received over 80 percent of His messages and perhaps the most significant.

The result is that nearly everything written in this book was revealed by God or supported by the Bible. The few exceptions and my personal opinions are clearly marked as such in the text.

1.4. The Importance of the Revelations

In truth, God's revelations are like fresh bread to the believer's spirit, which Pastor James Mc Innes of Union Church in Moravia, San Jose, Costa Rica, once described them. They come in answer to questions. They are clearly, directed to fill major gaps and build up a stronger commitment to God for us as believers. They can also serve as a platform that offers answers to unbelievers to lead them closer to God.

1.5. Revelations and Answers to Some of This Age's Big Questions

The revelations in this book provide answers to many of the questions that people have been asking. Most of all, they offer answers to some of the questions that many believers, even those who possess profound knowledge of the Word of God, are still asking. Many of them reveal the very mystery of God. Here are some of the many questions that will receive clear answers in this book:

1. What was God's purpose in creating humankind?
2. Why did God create an infinite universe?
3. Why was the devil envious of humankind?
4. How can we explain the mystery of the holy Trinity?
5. If neither the universe nor anything else in the world can contain God, how can the human heart contain Him?
6. How can God live fully and simultaneously in the hearts of millions of believers but still be one God?
7. Where is a human's spiritual heart located?
8. Where is the human soul located?
9. What material or essence is God using to build His holy temple, which is also, called, His holy dwelling, the bride of Christ, or the body of Christ?
10. What are the first and second deaths of the human being?
11. Why did the coming of Jesus not meet the expectations of the people of Israel, who were under the yoke of the Roman Empire?
12. What two historical events occurred simultaneously with the fall of Adam and Eve?
13. What does it mean to love God?
14. Why doesn't God, defeats the devil and get rid of evil and sin in the world, once, and for all?
15. Who were God's first children?

16. Why was it necessary for Paradise to exist, and who "lived" there?
17. Where are Enoch and Elijah who were, swept up by God? Are they in heaven with the Lord?
18. Why are all believers Israelites and children of Abraham?
19. What is the only thing in creation that God gave up to exercise His sovereignty?
20. What is a person's only real possession?
21. What is death? How many kinds of death are there?
22. Why is there no physical death from the spiritual standpoint?
23. What is the relationship between the Holy Spirit and the souls of people who receive Jesus Christ into their hearts?
24. What happens between the Holy Spirit and the souls of believers when they depart from this world?
25. When did Jesus achieve His two victories over death?
26. What is the mystery of the sacrificial blood? What is the difference between animal sacrifice and the sacrifice of Jesus, the Son of God?
27. Why is Jesus the firstborn from among the dead?
28. What is the kingdom of God?
29. Where is the kingdom of God and how far away is it from believers?

30. Why does God call himself "I Am"?
31. How does God gather and integrate His believers to shape His new dwelling place? This is the same thing as the church, the body of Christ, or the bride of the Lamb.
32. What is the name of the children of God's mother?
33. If believers are children of God, how can they come together and become the bride of the Lamb, but each one is still a child of God?
34. What is the New Jerusalem?
35. What did God mean when He said that David was a man after His own heart?
36. Why do today's believers mostly lack the power that the early Christians had?
37. Are the devil and Satan the same thing?
38. What is the difference between God the Alpha and God the Omega?
39. Why does the doctrine of pantheism find fulfillment in God alone, both as God the Alpha and as God the Omega?
40. Will people ever become God?
41. What is the believer's "time machine"?
42. Why is the Universe an apparition or a gigantic fantasy?

God gave us many revelations to uncover His mystery and in the process, answered these and other questions and concerns, which are in this book.

Before moving on, I would like to clear up a few matters to improve the understanding of this material.

1. The generic terms man and son that appear here, in the biblical sense include both men and women. In fact, the concept of gender, when meaning male and female, is a natural or earthly concept, which God created for the process of procreation or multiplication of the human race. It is a mechanism for the production of His potential sons and daughters. The human spirit, however, has no sex. It is neither male nor female, but spirit. Aware of today's growing sensitivity regarding gender, I want to clarify this.
2. This book uses the term *believer* as a synonym of the term *Christian* or *child of God.*
3. It is also important to point out to clarify that not all the truths recorded here are new, some are already known, they are in the Bible; but they serve as a foundation or reference for the understanding of these revelations. Each reader will then have to decide for himself what is new and what is already, known to him from everything contained in these pages.

4. It is also important to acknowledge, that not all the truths found here are entirely new. Some are in the Bible. They are included here as a base or reference point for explaining the revelations. As you peruse these pages, you must decide for yourself what is new and what you already know.

The value and perhaps the greatest significance of this book—this is my own view and not revealed by God—is that it stands as a body of revelations that are offered all in one place. They are there in the hope that they will help cleanse, revitalize, and breathe new life into the hearts of all people who are open and willing to take a deeper look at the only reality, which, been unseen, often escapes the understanding of many of us when our natural senses interfere with our spiritual understanding.

Chapter 2

GOD THE ONE IN THREE

The Alpha, First, and Only God

In the beginning, there was only God. He was alone in His three persons: Father, Son, and Holy Spirit. There was no one and nothing else. This is the reason that in the beginning, He was God the Alpha. He was the first and only God, who was one God in three persons. God was in His own dwelling place. He dwelt in himself and lived inside His own heart. There were no heavens, Earth, or universe. There was only God.

2.1. God's Plan

In the beginning, before the creation of the universe and foundation of the world, God conceived and designed a plan. God's plan was to make descendants for himself. He wanted to give himself a lineage and a house so that He could found a family. One of His purposes for having a family was to pour himself into it. To deposit His own essence into a family that would compose of a wife and children. Thus, God wanted descendants who would be an extension or a multiplication of himself. This could happen only if His lineage was rooted and anchored in holiness and love. It would be a family made up of God as Father, His bride as mother, and His children. The plan was for His family to become the same triangle of perfect love that existed between God the Father, God the Son, and God the Holy Spirit—the three persons of God, the one in three.

2.2. God's Holy, Royal Family

God's purpose was to found a family into which He could pour, express, and multiply himself, transforming every child into a priest and royal who would reign with Him for eternity. As God made plans to found His family line, He needed His bride and children to be as holy as He is. While sharing His essence, He wanted them not be exactly as himself but to have features that were different from His own.

Likewise, it is necessary for us, as His children, to be part of God as Father and His bride as mother, and that the two of them together, God and his bride, would be one, one single Spirit. This explains why God, who was echoing His own heavenly plan, His own family, decided that in earthly marriage, the man and the woman would become one flesh. Look at Mark 10:7–8:

> The Lord said, “For this reason a man will leave his father and mother and be united to his wife, **and the two will become one flesh**. So they are no longer two, but one flesh.” (Mark 10:7-8).

Therefore, even before the foundation of the world, God himself conceived and created the institution of family.

God also decided that His family, which consisted of His bride and His children, would simultaneously become His holy temple, His new dwelling place. One of His plans was and is to cease dwelling inside himself and live in the new home that He´s building. **This is the reason why God created humankind, to be or become part of his family, a family into which he intends to pour himself, express himself, and multiply himself**. It´s that simple. Because God, the heavenly architect, engineer, and perfect planner, thought it out before creating His people. He worked out a range of very detailed and special preparations to accommodate the masterpieces of His creation—his human, male and female.

These plans and preparations included creating the universe and everything in it. It was a majestic work made for the purpose of, representing a reality that was different from God’s own, and that at the same time, it would stand as a testimony to His majesty, grandeur, and splendor. The creation would also serve as a place for His people to live and settle, easing and facilitating their physical or natural existence.

2.3. Human Free Will

God made another extraordinary decision as part of His plans. He decided to subject the formation of His family to human will or decision. They would decide whether to love and accept or disobey and reject Him and His offer to form part of God's holy royal family. In so doing, God placed conditions and restrictions on himself, self-imposing limits according to the decision that His people would make. This is the reason why from the very beginning, God worked to create His people as righteous, perfect, and having the free will and freedom to choose.

God gave them rule over their free will. He blocked himself from exercising sovereignty over the people, insofar as their wills were concerned, which as we will see is the same thing as the human soul. My own view, which is not God's revelations, is that God understood there would be little value in creating people who without free will, were obliged or forced to love him, and had no other choice but to become part of His family. God knew that He could avail himself of His position as God and force this family, wife, and children to love him, but at the same time, His very essence is love, which does not take things by force or impose conditions.

In his letter to Philemon, the apostle Paul described the same spirit whereby God gave free will and did not force humankind to be His children, even though He could have.

> I would have liked to keep him with me so that he could take your place in helping me while I am in chains for the gospel. **But I did not want to do anything without your consent so any favor you do would not seem forced but would be voluntary**. (Philemon 13–14).

The free will that the Lord created in His people was a matter of such importance to Him, that, He wanted to be certain that it would be, used freely, and without coercion or imposition from himself. Therefore, God planned and created a different reality, which was the opposite of His own so that His creatures would have another choice available as an alternative to himself.

Part of this other option was for His people to exercise their free will in the physical or natural world with all its toils. People could make a clear decision to obey God, their creator, or consume themselves with the troubles of this world. In short, they could choose between the creator and His creation.

Therefore, God created the universe, which represents a visible reality, as an alternative to himself, which represents an invisible reality.

In short, God created a magnificent universe to enhance His own greatness. Also immense and majestic as a way of exposing the human being to a reality contrary to His own, to serve as a counterweight to himself; consequently, it constitutes an alternative for the exercise of man's free will.

2.4. The Tripartite Essence of the Human Creature

Once God had created the universe and everything in it, He set out to create His human masterpiece—the man and the woman. He created them with a three-part essence:

1. He made them as part of the Creator or part of himself, in His image and likeness, and akin to His own perfect, eternal spiritual essence.
2. He made them as part of His creation, that is, the universe, which is a physical, natural, and temporal essence.
3. God created humankind with a third essence that is different from those two. He imparted a soul as gift to His human creatures. The soul is the only one of the three essences that actually belongs to human being. His free will is expressed through it.

Take a look at Proverbs 16:1.

> **To humans belong the plans of the heart**, but from the Lord comes the proper answer of the tongue. (Proverbs 16:1).

God thus created His people as a trinity. One part is comprised of God himself, the Spirit of God. A second part is the universe itself inside them, their physical bodies. The third part is free and independent, their soul, a special spiritual essence that would allow people to follow the inclinations of their hearts and choose their own final destiny.

2.5. The Ultimate Purpose of Creation

This means that all existence, things both material and spiritual, is the result of God's creation and serves a single essential purpose: to facilitate and foster the building of God's family, His bride, and His many children. Taken as a body, these children will in turn, be His holy temple, God's new dwelling place. We see it described in Ephesians 2:19–22.

> Consequently, you are no longer foreigners and strangers, but fellow citizens with God's people, **and also members of his household**, built on

> the foundation of the apostles and prophets, with Christ Jesus himself as the chief cornerstone. In him the whole building is joined together and rises to become **a holy temple** in the Lord. And in him you too are being built together to become **a dwelling in which God lives** by his Spirit. (Ephesians 2:19-22).

As we saw earlier, God has always been His own temple and dwelt within His own heart. Before the foundation of the world, one of the decisions He made was to build a family that would become His new dwelling place and temple, which would take shape inside himself. This family is being fashioned out of the clean, pure, redeemed, transformed, and revived souls of all who believe in Jesus Christ and who are saved by Him. **Therefore, God's new temple is a work in progress and fully under construction**.

Jesus Christ, God´s firstborn is the first building block, the first precious stone of God´s new temple, of His new dwelling place. The saved in Jesus Christ are the rest of the precious stones of His temple. **Thus, the material that is being used, to build God's new dwelling place is the human soul. Soul of those redeemed, transformed, and revived by the blood of Jesus.**

God's ultimate purpose and intent for everything in creation is to bring about His plan, in one way or another.

In brief, all the creation serves God and His purposes. Romans 11:36 and Psalms 119:91 reaffirm it as follows:

> For from him and through him and for him are all things. To him be the glory forever! Amen. (Romans 11:36).

> Your laws endure to this day, for **all things serve you**. (Psalms 119:91).

While God's desire is for all people to be part of His family, they still have the free exercise of their will. Although some will choose to join Him, others will turn Him down. All of us, without exception, are the facilitators of the process of forming His family; that is, building His holy temple and His new dwelling place. Nothing and no one can opt out and escape from God's will. Everyone has the choice to accept or reject God's offer to join His family, but what no one can do is to step away from God's plans, because we all, without exception, are placed in His framework.

2.6. The Defining Trait of God's Family

God is love, and been love one of His main attributes, one of the main conditions that God sets for building His family is that it must be founded on love. There must be love among the father, mother, and children. It is the reason why God has loved us devotedly and unconditionally from the very beginning.

God desires for His bride and children to love Him above all else and to Him first. God wants to establish the same triangle of perfect love and harmony that exists within the divine Trinity (Father, Son, and Holy Spirit) with His family. All that is necessary is that His people become believers and love God. As a result, His spouse, also known as the bride of the Lamb or the church, will love Him as well. Remember that the bride of the Lamb is the composite of all redeemed, transformed, and revived souls of the believers. **Thus, the main trait of God's family is that it´s rooted and anchored in the very love of the Father**.

Chapter 3

THE ROLE OF THE DEVIL

To repeat, the sole purpose of creation is to serve and facilitate God's plans—to form His family and build His holy dwelling place. The devil is also part of creation, and without a doubt, he is, also part of God's plans and purposes.

In the absence of the devil, there would be no evil or sin and people, would not be faced with the necessary choice of exercising their free wills, which again, is an essential condition for becoming part of God's holy, royal family. It may seem paradoxical, but that is why, the devil is an integral part of God's purposes.

In fact, the devil and his armies are the essential scaffolding on which God builds His holy dwelling place. Like all scaffolding, they will meet their end, when they are finally, ripped away and discarded. They help build God's holy dwelling place by holding out a different option, which will allow God's people to exercise their free will. Nevertheless, in the end, they will be discarded and they won't be a part of God's eternal home.

God has allowed Satan to pursue his evil ways as a strategy to work out His fundamental purposes. He allows His people to choose to use their free will for good or evil; that is, life or death. God will always meet His own goals, and He sometimes does so by using the enemy and the evil ones. Judas Iscariot is a clear example, as Jesus says in John 17:12:

> While I was with them, I protected them and kept them safe by that name you gave me. None has been lost **except the one doomed to destruction so that Scripture would be fulfilled**". (John 17:12).

God used Judas to fulfill His own purpose in Jesus. He did the same thing with Joseph's brothers, the sons of Jacob. He bent their own evil impulses and sent Joseph to Egypt, where He would prepare the way for the children of Israel to arrive and seek shelter during the famine that struck the land. Look at Genesis 45:4–5:

> Then Joseph said to his brothers, "Come close to me." When they had done so, he said, "I am your brother Joseph, the one you sold into Egypt! **And now, do not be distressed and do not be angry with yourselves for selling me here, because it was to save lives that God sent me ahead of you**. (Genesis 45:4-5).

Another example is the case of the Egyptian pharaoh. God used him by hardening his heart so that God could display His grandeur and great power before the Hebrews and in the process, build their character. Today, God still uses the enemy to offer us another option and an alternative to himself, and in the process, He tests us and builds our character, perseverance, and above all, our faith. Our responsibility, therefore, is to persevere in the faith, cultivate it, and make it grow so that we can resist the constant onslaught of the devil and defeat him with our faith.

Anyone who has faith and is obedient to God can resist the evil that is, personified, in the devil. The devil always flees such resistance, as stated clearly in James 4:7:

> Submit yourselves therefore to God. **Resist the devil and he will flee from you**. (James 4:7).

The devil is persistent. Therefore, over, and over, he often tests the human character, by using any number of stratagems and tactics. The story of Job is everyone's story, in one way or another. It gives a clear picture of the devil's aggressiveness. In many cases, Satan wins the battle, ends up undermining the very character of his victims, destroys them, and eventually takes control of their souls.

Job is God's example to show us what our character and attitude to adversity should be like. He teaches us about the character and perseverance that we need to develop and hold onto our faith in the Lord, no matter what happens and in every circumstance.

Some of the trials we must undergo can be devastating, as Job learned. Ours may not be so, overwhelming as what he experienced. Nevertheless, everyone, without exception, undergoes trials. Even Jesus was tested and tempted. No one is exempt because every human is required to exercise their gift of free will as a prerequisite to be qualified to enter into God´s family, His new dwelling place. When people face with two mutually exclusive options as to choose between good and evil, or life and death, they have to exercise their free will.

In short, not even the devil can escape from God's plans and purposes. Instead, he is a key part of God's master plan to found a family and build His holy dwelling place. **This explains why God has not eliminated the devil once, and for all, and with him, the evil and sin of the world. Because, until God finishes the process of shaping His family, the devil will continue to be useful and will remain present.**

However, once the Lord finishes the building of His family, His temple, His new dwelling place, the devil will be removed permanently. Because by then, his role as "scaffolding" will be over and, as befits all scaffolding, once construction is complete, it tosses out forever.

3.1. Who Is Satan?

The Bible often refers to the devil by the name of Satan. As a result, many come to believe that the devil and Satan are one, and the same. In a sense, they are, nevertheless, let´s clarify certain aspects.

3.1.1. Who Satan really is?

Satan is someone who serves as stumbling block or a temptation to lure people into sin. Let´s look at the discussion between Jesus and Peter in Matthew 16:22–23.

> Peter took him aside and began to rebuke him. "Never, Lord!" he said. "This shall never happen to you!" Jesus turned and said to Peter, "**Get behind me, Satan**! You are a stumbling block to me; you do not have in mind the concerns of God, but merely human concerns." (Matthew 16;22-23).

Jesus openly called Peter "Satan," but Peter was not the devil.

The devil is called "Satan" quite often. Because the devil is the most Satan of all satans. That is because the devil is a Satan par excellence. It must be understood however, that when conditions are ripe, any person can become a Satan at any particular time, even if that person is a veritable saint.

Chapter 4

THE HUMAN SOUL

We know that God created His people perfect, gave them free will, and made sure that they would need to use it as a requirement to be part of God's family. This free will is the soul that God placed in His human creatures.

When He decided to found His family, God did not want it to be the same as himself or just like Him. Therefore, He chose to create a spiritual essence that was different from himself to stand as the foundation for His family. That essence is the human soul. In other words, God did not want to marry himself. He did not want to take a bride who was himself, made of himself, or had His exact same nature and very essence. Therefore, God created the human soul, and gave it to His people, limited His own sovereignty over it, and left it in their hands. However, He added one necessary, indispensable, specific provision. That the human soul would have the capacity to be assimilated by God′s essence and cohabit or dwell with God's Spirit.

4.1. Features of the Human Soul

As we saw, God created His people with a soul (spiritual essence). This soul is a type of trinity that is made of three manifestations or essences—mind, emotions, and will. Even as the Trinity of God consists of one God who is present in all His fullness in three persons, so the human soul is just one, and is also present in all its fullness in each of these three essences or manifestations. More specifically, people's minds hold within them the fullness of their emotions and will. Their emotions fully contain their minds and will. Their will fully contain their minds and emotions. The fullness of the soul itself is contained in the three essences. Each one of these essences of the soul contains the fullness of the other two and of the soul.

Even as God is one, the human soul is one. The soul bestows our free will. The soul is located in the human heart. The following comparison summarizes it. We say that God is one and that He comprises a trinity of Father, Son, and Holy Spirit. Each of the three persons is present simultaneously in the other two. God's fullness is always present in each of His three persons. In the same way, the human soul is one, and it comprises a trinity of mind, emotions, and will. Each of the three essences is present simultaneously in the other two, and the fullness of the soul is always present in each of the essences. It is also important to remember that every person's soul is unique and singular, because that is what makes each person a unique creation of God, never to be duplicated.

By the way, regarding the above and from the Divine standpoint, no person is ordinary, even if he or she thinks and acts as such. The foregoing is because, each, and every one of us is a masterpiece, unique and unrepeatable of God's creation. Therefore, it is impossible for a person to be ordinary; rather when someone thinks he or she is, and consequently, acts as such, that offends the Lord by despising His masterpiece.

4.2. The Trinity of God and Its Relationship with the Trinity of the Soul

There is a one-to-one correspondence between the three persons of the Trinity of God and the three parts or essences that make up the trinity of the human soul. This means that there is an affinity or a counterpart between the essences of the human trinity and the persons of the divine Trinity. This is how it looks:

- God's Holy Spirit fervently desires the human will.
- The Son, Jesus Christ, fervently desires the human emotions.
- The Father fervently desires the human mind.

God created humankind with the potential to control their soul. However, when life unfolds, and they look towards God, and turn their backs on Him, this potential capacity will or will not grow to a real capacity to hold control and steward their soul.

The human soul was created to honor God. As it happens, if you wish to control your soul, you need to honor God. Honor Him with:

1. Your thoughts (mind),
2. Your feelings (emotions), and
3. Your intentions (will).

Therefore, when your soul enters into harmony and fellowship with the Spirit of God, you will find it easier to exercise control and stewardship over your soul.

4.3. Your Most Precious Possession: Your Soul

People tend not to think much about their souls. Paradoxically, it is by far your most precious possession. **Indeed, it is your only possession**. This is because the Spirit of God, whom you receive when you confess Christ as your Lord and Savior, does not belong to you but to God. Your body, the natural or physical tabernacle, belongs to the universe and more specifically, to the earth, to which it always returns. By contrast, **your soul is your own. It**

is a gift from God and your only real possession, your real treasure. Therefore, your soul is the only thing that you can exercise control over to decide your final destiny.

The human soul is the most precious thing to God, and this is what He desires from you. He desires it fervently and passionately.

> **That is the reason why, it is true to say that a natural person is in reality his soul**.

God gave all people the potential to control their own souls and exercise dominion over them. This is not so simple because the devil also desires every person's soul. He will never stop fighting for it as long as that person is still in this world. The clash is inevitable because, it is part of the battle all human beings need to fight if they wish to exercise their free will.

This is why we all need to remember that the war is real, and that, its outcome has everlasting consequences that are unmatched by anything else in our lives, and that so long as we remain in this world, we must persevere, fight, and never give up. This war can take many shapes. It is not always obvious to us. Therefore, is one of the most serious challenges we face.

If you keep God at a distance, you will have very little hope of controlling and exercising stewardship and dominion over your soul. If instead, you choose to draw near to God and submit to Him, your potential to exercise dominion over your soul will be clear and unquestionable.

When you distance yourself from God, whether you realize it or not, you grant the enemy access to your soul and control over it. Nearness to God and the fullness of the Holy Spirit give you power, authority, and wisdom to submit your soul and to exercise dominion over it.

Moreover, the only thing in creation over which God does not hold sovereignty is human free will; that is, the human soul.

Accordingly, your soul is the only thing that you *can* hold sovereignty and control over.

This is the reason that when you draw near to God and learn to dominate and take lordship over your soul, namely, your thoughts, emotions, and will, you will develop the great power and authority that the Lord holds ready for those who believe and obey Him.

4.4. The Ultimate Mission for Humankind

As explained above, your most valuable possession is your soul, God fervently desires the human soul, and the devil is after it too. Therefore, it is not possible to overemphasize the fact that each human being's primary mission in life is to develop the ability to exercise dominion and control over his or her own soul. With the firm purpose of setting it aside, caring for it, reserving it, and finally handing it over to God. In other words, **our ultimate mission in life is to surrender our souls to the Lord**, to return it back to Him as a gift because He is who gave it originally.

4.5. God's Holy Spirit and the Human Soul

When you accept Jesus Christ as your Lord and Savior, God's Holy Spirit enters your heart and attaches to your soul. This is the beginning of a relationship, an active cohabitation, or a co-inherency between them. This relationship involves mutual indwelling between the Spirit of God and the human soul.

John 14:17, 23 corroborates the fact with the following words:

> The Spirit of truth. The world cannot accept him, because it neither sees him nor knows him. But you know him, **for he lives with you and will be in you**. Jesus replied, "Anyone who loves me will obey my teaching. My Father will love them, **and we will come to them and make our home with them**. (John 14:17. 23).

Note that the Lord did not say, we will make our home in them but with them, which means a mutual dwelling.

4.5.1. What Is Co-Inherency or Cohabitation?

The following is the definition of the term co-inherency or cohabitation, which will have applied, throughout this book:

> Co-inherence or cohabitation **is the mutual coexistence or the active relationship of mutual indwelling,** one in the other, between the Holy Spirit of God and the soul of man.

So when the Spirit of God enters your heart, He begins to live with you. The Holy Spirit and your soul merge into a single spirit and create an indivisible, indissoluble union between the two. When this happens, the human soul changes its very essence and adopts the essence of the Holy Spirit, which is the essence of God. This is clear in 1st. Corinthians 6:17.

> But whoever is united with the Lord **is one with him in spirit**. (1st. Corinthians 6:17).

A form of marriage takes place between them, and a process begins in which the believer's soul comes to know God more and more through the Holy Spirit. It is hard to comprehend that the Almighty himself begins to cohabit and live together with the believer's soul and accordingly, with a human being. Thus, the miracle of co-inherency or cohabitation is that the Holy Spirit simultaneously dwells within the believer's soul and the believer's soul dwells within the Holy Spirit. Consider what the Lord says in John 14:20.

> On that day you will realize that **I am in my Father, and you are in me, and I am in you**. (John 14:20).

This relationship of co-inherency or cohabitation on Earth therefore, constitutes a pledge or a small but significant down payment on the eventual co-inherency between God and His family (bride and children) throughout eternity. When the Spirit of God enters the human heart, He connects with the soul and revives it, kindles it, and breathes new life into it. Remember that until now, the soul was spiritually dead and in darkness, but at this instant, the soul shines forth, and it is born into life. Only then does a person acquire the essence of God. The human becomes the image and likeness of God as it was back at the beginning during creation.

This relationship of co-inherency or cohabitation between the Spirit of God and the believer's soul creates a type of miniature mutual tabernacle. In this mutual dwelling and intertwining, the human soul gradually assimilates the divine conditions of the Holy Spirit but not the contrary. Consequently, the believer's soul begins the process of transformation so that it can undertake the journey into the kingdom of God.

This process of assimilation and preparation continues throughout your time in this world. It ends only when you leave the world behind. When you complete your natural life cycle, the Holy Spirit returns to God and takes His earthly home—your revived soul—with Him.

The human soul cannot be perfected or flourish in the absence of fellowship and co-inherency with the Holy Spirit. This is why God sent His Holy Spirit to perfect your soul and allow it to flourish.

Finally, it would be a mistake to overlook the great miracle that occurs when the Holy Spirit—Almighty God himself—takes up residence within the human heart. In 1st. Kings 8:27, King Solomon declares the following:

> But will God really dwell on earth? **The heavens, even the highest heaven, cannot contain you**. How much less this temple I have built! (1st. Kings 8:27).

King Solomon spoke with astonishment because the house He had built for God could not contain Him.

If the entire universe cannot contain God, how can the human heart fully hold Him? So great is His love and desire for His people, that God performs the miracle of allowing His fullness to dwell within the hearts of believers. God does this by creating a very special spiritual essence, the human soul, which does not belong to the universe, nor form any part of it, but it is a spiritual essence that under certain circumstances is capable of containing God.

The explanation of this miracle is because only God can contain himself and that He cannot depart from himself.

> Therefore, in order for the Lord to dwell in the human heart, His Holy Spirit transforms and converts the human soul to the very essence of God, merging with it indivisible and indissolubly. In this way, the soul, converted to the essence of God, acquires the capacity to contain God, because in reality, it is God containing himself.

This is why King Solomon's cry that the universe could not contain God is still true and valid today. As it happens, God, the only one who is able to contain himself, is not of this world. Therefore, He is not of this universe. This is truly marvelous! Don´t you agree.

For all these reasons, when the Lord converts a human heart into His own dwelling place, He actually transfers heaven into the believer's heart. Heaven is no longer a faraway, mysterious, remote, and unknowable place. In fact, it lies within the believer's own heart because heaven is the very presence of God. Heaven is where God is.

The curious thing is that although believers know the Lord dwells within their hearts, all too often, we describe Him as a God who is very far from us and in an unfathomable, unknowable heaven, when in fact, the Lord, Almighty God, is within our hearts, which He has transformed into His dwelling place. Astonishing!

Chapter 5

ADAM AND EVE

Perfect, Immortal, Spiritual Beings

We will now consider the environment and conditions in which God made His human creatures, Adam and Eve. He fashioned them to be righteous and perfect beings—spiritual, holy, immortal, and therefore, eternal. He created them in His own image and likeness, out of His Holy Spirit. This means that they were made of His own essence, created as children of God. **Consequently, they were God's first children on Earth**. Luke 3:38 talks about this in the genealogy of Jesus.

> …the son of Enosh, the son of Seth, the son of Adam, **the son of God**. (Luke 3:38).

Adam and Eve existed in a perfect circle of pure life because everything in them was life. God created them with free will, though, and gave them power and authority over everything on the earth—animals, beasts, fish, birds, and plants—in short, everything. There was no pain, sin, death, or physical labor because God gave them the power, authority, and capacity to rule, lead, and exercise dominion over His creation through the words express through their thought.

It is important to understand that Adam and Eve were pure of heart. Their hearts were free of evil thoughts or negative emotions. Such things were unknown and did not exist. This included negative emotions such as greed, anger, jealousy, hatred, and superstition. Spirits, such as the spirit of fear, simply had no place in their hearts.

When God created Adam and Eve with free will, He made sure they could genuinely use it. He had to offer them other options so that they could choose freely. He set before them life and goodness, as well as death and evil. This is clear in Deuteronomy 30:15.

> See, I set before you today **life and prosperity, death and destruction**. (Deuteronomy 30:15).

His instructions were quite specific as He ordered them *not to eat the fruit of the tree of the knowledge of good and evil.* As a result, Adam and Eve now had the opportunity to exercise their free will and either obey or disobey God.

5.1. The Fall of Adam and Eve

Adam and Eve chose to disobey God, and in so doing, they discarded Him as their Lord in favor of a new master, Satan. Thus was their perfect circle of life broken and converted into an imperfect *straight line or linear continuum*, where life and goodness were at one end and death and evil, originally absent from their lives, were at the other. Therefore, with the fall of Adam and Eve, human existence has become a sort of *imperfect linear continuum*, with life and goodness and death and evil at its two ends.

In the Garden of Eden, Adam and Eve had communicated with all the beings in existence as a normal routine, and the creatures communicated with them. This communication took place via the humans' supra conscious.[1]

5.1.1. Satan's Deceit

Satan was jealous of Adam and Eve, unable to accept the fact that while they were spiritual beings, they would simultaneously have free will and the ability to choose for themselves. No angel had ever had this quality of free will, given to him, by God. He set out to deceive them in hopes that they would lose God's favor. He started watching them closely in the Garden and looking for a way to deceive and lure them into disobeying God. His observations paid off when he realized that the one he really needed to deceive was Adam, as the head of the pair, and that he could get to Adam through Eve.

---

[1] This text will use the term *supra conscious* because *subconscious* would be a misnomer.

Satan devised his plan. He would establish a very good relationship with Eve and win her trust as a means of getting to Adam through her. He decided to seek her out, communicate with her, and start building a relationship of trust.

The serpent is an allegory that depicts Satan communicating with Eve. Ever astute and persistent, the serpent (the devil) took the time to cultivate a friendly relationship with Eve. They chatted about the entitlements and constraints on the fruits of the trees that she and Adam could eat from in the garden. Then, Satan began to feed Eve's heart with new emotions, all of them negative. He achieved something else as well. He undermined the love that Eve felt for God, and thus, he weakened her obedience to Him.

Because of this, negative feelings invaded Eve's heart for the first time and began to contaminate and corrupt it. The first negative emotions were:

- Greed
- Envy
- Superstition

5.1.2. Greed

Satan convinced Eve that God did not want her and Adam to eat the fruit of the tree of the knowledge of good and evil because if they did, they would be like God. This led Eve to begin coveting God's nature in her heart. She wanted to be like God.

5.1.3. Envy

Envy is the other negative emotion that blended with greed in Eve's heart because she began to envy God and His condition as God.

5.1.4. Superstition

The third negative emotion that Eve began to experience in her heart and that continued to contaminate her was superstition. It came when she believed that by eating the fruit of the tree of the knowledge of good and evil, she would attain the nature of God and be like Him.

After several encounters with Satan the serpent, Eve began to experience these new feelings, which eventually contaminated her heart. It became contaminated and corrupt. One of the most important positive emotions began to recede from her heart: love, specifically, her love for God. So mired in deep confusion, Eve and Adam began to exercise their free will and choose the option of disobeying God.

5.2. Adam and Eve Lose the Image and Likeness of God

It is very important to remember that before their fall, Adam and Eve had not activated their five natural senses, such as the ones we have today. That is because they didn't need them. This is because their supra-senses (spiritual senses) were very active and well developed.

God had foreseen everything, though, even the possibility that His creatures might disobey Him and have their spiritual nature degraded to a natural condition. Therefore, He created the human being with both spiritual and natural senses. At the beginning, their natural senses weren't activated. However, when Adam and Eve fall in disobedient, and they sinned, they lost their spiritual nature, and consequently, they were downgraded to a natural condition. Therefore, their natural senses were activated. This change in status is significant because the spiritual senses are fully reliable while the natural senses are deceitful and treacherous.

With the fall of Adam and Eve, therefore, two critical, historical events took place:

1. They lost the image and likeness of God, and
2. Their natural senses were activated.

They lost the image and likeness of God because when they disobeyed God and sinned, they lost their holiness and experienced spiritual death as the Spirit of God immediately departed from them. The Spirit of God left their hearts, which had become contaminated and corrupt.

Let´s remember that God does not conjoin with sin or the sinful nature, which was Adam and Eve´s newly acquired nature. God withdrew His essence, which was incompatible with corruption and sin.

The second fundamental historical fact—the activation of their natural senses—occurred because when the Spirit of God departed from their hearts, they lost their spiritual natures and became natural beings who were distant from God. Their natural senses needed to be activate if they were to live and function in their new condition.

God's Word says that when they sinned, their eyes opened and only then, did they see that they were naked. This reveals something about the activation of their natural senses. The Word also says that they frightened by God's voice. We see the description in Genesis 3:7–10.

> Then **the eyes of both of them were opened, and they realized they were naked**; so they sewed fig leaves together and made coverings for themselves. **Then the man and his wife heard the sound of the Lord God** as he was walking in the garden in the cool of the day, and they hid from the Lord God among the trees of the garden. But the Lord God called to the man, "Where are you?"

> He answered, "**I heard you in the garden, and I was afraid**, because I was naked; so I hid." (Genesis 3:7-10).

Only after Adam and Eve had sinned, their natural eyes opened. For the first time, they saw that they were naked. When the Lord God spoke to them for the first time in an audible voice in the garden, they heard Him with their natural sense of hearing. Because it was new and unknown to them, it awakened fear. Therefore, it was under these conditions that Adam and Eve first experienced the presence of the spirit of fear, which is one of the most effective spirits in the world of darkness. It triggers the most negative emotional reactions known to humankind.

Their hearts were contaminated with the same powerful, negative emotions that continue to contaminate human hearts today and distance them from God. Other negative emotions, such as greed, envy, and superstition, are the emotional consequences of the spirit of fear.

5.3. From Living, Perfect, Spiritual Beings to Dead, Imperfect Humans

God created the man and the woman as perfect spiritual beings by placing His Own Spirit within them. This meant that they contained the triune nature of spirit, soul, and body. After the fall, Adam and Eve lost their spiritual condition. So, they were downgraded to the status of natural humans, who were imperfect, sinful, and spiritually dead.

Adam and Eve committed the original sin of disobedience, and thereafter, all people were born without the Spirit of God in their hearts nor the image and likeness of God. Therefore, dating back to the fall of Adam and Eve, people have lost their full nature as spirit, soul, and body that was replaced by an incomplete nature containing only soul and body.

We tend to talk about the human spirit, but as we will see, it is actually the human soul, which is not material but spiritual in essence. For those who do not have the Spirit of God in their hearts, their misnamed spirit is actually the soul.

In short, when Adam and Eve fell, they lost their supra-senses, and their natural senses were activated. They fell from a state of a full life to a state of sin and death. They moved from a position of absolute existential certainty to one of total uncertainty and dependence on their natural senses, which are unreliable and deceptive. This is the same state that humans, as natural people, are in today. It is a state in which whatever seems to be, almost never is; whatever we believe we see, does not exist, and whatever we feel, is not consistent with reality. This is the world where natural humans live. It is a phantom world of appearances, deception, uncertainty, sin, and death.

5.4. And Death Is Born

Even though, originally, Adam and Eve had physical bodies, they were spiritual, immortal, and eternal beings. After their fall, however, they became natural, mortal beings, who were governed by their natural senses.

It may sound strange to speak of the birth of death, but it is important to understand that when God created Adam and Eve, death did not exist. Death was born with the sin of Adam and Eve's disobedience.

After the fall of Adam and Eve, this original, primary sin would pursue all humans to come, for all time. This is why, after that original sin that took Adam and Eve to spiritual death, every person is born dead, born in sin and darkness, separate from God, with the exception of Jesus Christ.

We are born spiritually dead because there is no life in us and no light in our hearts. When we are born, the Spirit of God is neither with us nor in us. Therefore, spiritual death is the human condition at birth.

This is why powerful King Solomon prophesied about the future condition of believers when he said in Ecclesiastes 7:1:

> "A good name is better than fine perfume, **and the day of death better than the day of birth**. (Ecclesiastes 7:1).

Here, King Solomon draws a comparison to the day of birth when all are born dead in sin and darkness and utterly separated from God. Then when he speaks of the day of death, he makes prophetic reference to the death to sin that is possible with Christ when the soul joins with the life-giving Holy Spirit. In some sense, Solomon was pointing to the fact that a believer who is born also dies and that a believer who dies to sin lives. This is why he rightly stated that death is better than birth. It is because the Holy Spirit is life and to have the Spirit is to have life. The absence of the Spirit is death. So all humans except for Jesus Christ are born dead because of Adam and Eve's fall; that is, because of their original sin.

It is only when a person accepts Jesus Christ as Lord and Savior that he or she is reborn, this time into life. That person acquires spiritual life. He or she is being transformed from a natural being, who is incomplete and dead, into a new spiritual being, who is complete and alive.

A person, who is born to the Spirit of God, is changed to His essence. That individual makes a complete about-face—a 180-degree turn—passing from the state of death into the state of life. The Spirit of God becomes this person's primary essence, which marks the difference between life and death.

Anyone who is not born of the Spirit of God is an incomplete human being. A complete person, who is born from the Spirit of God, can be described differently as follows:

5.4.1. The Human as a Spirit or the Spiritual Self

Again, people are not born with spiritual natures, but they acquire this condition when they become believers by receiving Jesus Christ into their hearts. Once they acquire this nature, it becomes their primary essence (their spiritual self) because it gives them true and eternal life.

5.4.2. The Human as a Soul or the Soulish Self

People, are all differentiated from one another by their souls, which makes each one a unique masterpiece of God's creation and allows them to exercise their free will. The soulish self is the part of our makeup that really belongs to us, a gift from God to us, and it is the part that God fervently desires, and longs for us to surrender to Him.

5.4.3. The Human as a Body or the Physical Self

The physical part of our makeup—what we see in the mirror—is a sort of tabernacle where the other two parts and selves (spiritual and soulish) live. The physical self is the least important part of the human makeup. The temporary part that belongs to the earth is made of dust and returns to the ground when we depart from this world.

5.5. Adam and Eve and Their Supra-Senses

When the Spirit of God dwelt in the hearts of Adam and Eve, their supra-senses were fully developed. This condition made it possible for them to function at a higher and more spiritual level rather than the physical and natural level that we manage today. Adam and Eve communicated with God, each other, and the creation, using their supra-senses. They saw in visions and sensed spiritually, as all their senses were spiritual before the fall. The five natural senses we depend on so much today were not activated, which meant that Adam and Eve saw, smelled, heard, felt, and tasted by means of the spiritual senses in their supra conscious.

Adam and Eve natural sense were activated, when they sinned. With the passage of time as sin took over more and more territory, the human heart became increasingly hardened, and the spiritual senses atrophied.

The death and resurrection of Jesus Christ brought the possibility of a second birth for us all. It was a second birth into life, which would revive the human soul and allow people to recover their spiritual nature. With it, the fullness of their supra-senses would enable them to perceive events in the spiritual world, such as seeing visions. We see an example in Acts 11:5–6, where Peter describes his vision.

> I was in the city of Joppa praying, **and in a trance I saw a vision**. I saw something like a large sheet being let down from heaven by its four corners, and it came down to where I was.
>
> I looked into it and saw four-footed animals of the earth, wild beasts, reptiles, and birds. (Acts 11:5-6).

Once again, what is commonly known as the subconscious mind is what we call the supra conscious because unquestionably, the realm often known as the subconscious mind is a vastly higher sense, and therefore, it holds a higher rank than the conscious mind. It is a supra conscious that holds powerful spiritual qualities and a channel by which God speaks to the human heart.

Chapter 6

TRANSMISSION AND RECEPTION CHANNELS OF THE HUMAN SUPRA CONSCIOUS

Among other things, the human brain is a powerful receiving and transmitting station. The human supra conscious both transmits and receives according to the following features:

1. It transmits over a single channel. God, people and other spiritual being receive this transmission.
2. It received over two channels—a primary or main channel called the primary receiving channel (PRC) and a secondary channel called the secondary receiving channel (SRC).

The PRC is the channel where we receive communication exclusively from God while the SRC provides us with communication from all other supra conscious beings or brains, including the devil.

For example, God communicated with Adam and Eve over the PRC, and they received communication from one another over their SRC. They also received communication over the SRC from other beings that shared their communication capabilities, such as the animals in the Garden of Eden. This explains how the serpent, Satan, was able to communicate with Eve.

6.1. Features of the Secondary Receiving Channel

The SRC is a fully open channel, and we cannot close, block, or filter through it, unless we get positive thoughts and emotions and, consequently, the intentions of our will to dominate our hearts through our supra conscious. In this condition, our PRC is kept, fully open. When the PRC is fully open, the Spirit of God gives us the ability to control what we receive over the SRC.

Because of the relationship between the PRC and the SRC, anyone whose PRC is blocked loses all ability to control what comes in over the SRC. Under such conditions, people often find themselves at the mercy of the devil and his demonic hosts because they have stepped out from under God's covering. This is when many people slip into depression and can even reach the extreme action of suicide. Their instincts for self-preservation (their stream of life), have become very weak and is easily overcome by the demon-driven desire to stop living and let go of life.

Some people come to their senses at the very last minute and experience a powerful desire to live. This strong emotion and desire activate their supra conscious, which powerfully awakens and unblocks the reception in the PRC. Thus, the PRC resets and immediately revives the flow of life, which is, the instinct for self-preservation that saves the person from self-annihilation and inevitable eternal damnation.

When the PRC is open and life is flowing freely, God deploys great powers through His human instruments. This is when God's Word goes into action, as in Luke 10:19.

> Behold, **I have given you authority to tread upon serpents and scorpions, and over all the power of the enemy**; and nothing shall hurt you. (Luke 10:19).

6.2. The Instinct for Self-Preservation and the Primary Receiving Channel

The instinct for self-preservation is a sort of spirit or halo of life that God has instilled in His people. It is as a steady stream of life or a channel through which life flows continuously in us. This stream of life is what makes us cling so tightly to our natural life.

Another way to explain the instinct of self-preservation is to compare it to a cursor that runs from one end of a straight line to another, a linear continuum. Life is at one end, and death is at the other. A person who is far from God, and therefore, whose PRC is partially blocked; has the self-preservation cursor heading toward the dead-end of the linear continuum. However, when a believer is firmly anchored in God, the cursor heads closer towards the other extreme of the line where there is life, and the result is powerful to see.

The natural, incomplete person who is spiritually dead, unbelieving, or ungodly has a self-preservation instinct much like the small pilot light on a gas stove. So long as there is gas in the pipes and the valve is open, the pilot light continues burning whether the stove is on or off; therefore, the incomplete, natural person is as a gas stove that is off and cold, even though the pilot light is still burning. By contrast, the pilot light in a believer, a whole, spiritual person, has roared into a blazing flame because the stove is on, and produces light, heat, and full life.

The PRC is located in the human supra conscious. It remains lit and functioning at an optimal level in those who lead a life of obedience in accordance with the statutes and precepts of God. Sometimes the supra conscious begins to come under the influence of evil thoughts, and it is energized by negative emotions, which start to create a blockage in the PRC. It sickens, and the flow (the self-preservation instinct we are calling the pilot light) begins to weaken and flicker out. This is when the SRC starts to take primacy over the PRC.

Because God communicates with His people over the PRC while other beings, especially the devil, communicate over the SRC, the devil often takes advantage of a person's weak instinct for self-preservation. He steps up his communication with the supra conscious, sending evil thoughts, negative emotions, and even destructive impulses. His intention is to take possession of the supra conscious and hence, of the human soul.

People in this state have a weakened instinct for self-preservation. Such a condition can plunge you into a state of sorrow and depression. Under certain circumstances, it can lead to suicide. When the instinct for self-preservation in the supra conscious is blocked or the pilot light goes out, it leaves you under the power of evil thoughts and negative emotions, which are induced by the devil. He convinces you that life is not worth living and that it is better to die.

6.3. Depression

All those who are far from God, even knowing He exists—whether they are rich or poor, powerful or weak—whatever their condition, will suffer from some degree of sadness or depression due to the significant shrinkage of their instinct for self-preservation.

Sometimes an entire people and culture suffer from some degree of collective depression. These people not only deliberately insist on denying God but also in some cases, even rise up against Him. They are very different from other people or nations that, out of ignorance, do not know Him. In these cases, God tends to nurture the stream of life, making sure that they will have their chance to know Him and exercise their free will so that they can accept Him and be born to life or reject Him and continue to be spiritually dead.

This explains why some cultures see suicide as normal. Most of these people tend to have their PRC significantly blocked or diseased. The stream of life, that is, the instinct for self-preservation is weak, and the pilot light has nearly snuffed out. They feel indifferent toward life, and losing it becomes unimportant.

God works to keep the human PRC open, but many, by their own choice, block or disconnect their channel to avoid receiving the transmission. It is as if they tried to turn off or snuff out their conscience. Every one of us has the option to control the on-off switch and graduate our own PRC's level of intensity. This control switch is closely linked to the place that Almighty God occupies in each person's life.

If you, exercising your free will, choose to reject God, distance yourself from him, and move out from under His protection, you generally block your PRC, leaving only the SRC open. This is the way that the devil moves in and seizes the moment to set up a base in the human supra conscious, inside the very human heart. In such a state, a person can end up possessed by the devil and his demonic armies.

Chapter 7

FREE WILL, THE SOUL, AND THE HUMAN HEART

Free will is your ability to control your own thoughts, feelings, and will, that is, to control your soul. In reality, it is the God-given ability or freedom for you to choose whether you will surrender your soul to God or allow it be conquered by evil.

It is also humans' freedom to decide whether they want to be slaves to sin—a condition that will eventually lead to the final death—or be free forever. This freedom will take you to eternal life. Satan is waging a never-ending battle to win over humans' minds, emotions, and will and conquer the human soul. It explains why everyone must develop the ability and habit of controlling our own thoughts (minds), desires (emotions), and intentions (will).

All human beings must make a deliberate effort to learn to control their own minds and thoughts, discard undesirable thoughts, and choose the things they should think instead. You must learn to block evil thoughts and tell your heart what it must think. Never forget that God gave you full authority over your soul—your thoughts, feelings, and will.

Three different voices are generally murmuring in your inner thoughts, and you need to make a conscious effort to distinguish among them. These voices are

1. God's voice through the Holy Spirit.
2. The inner voice of your own thoughts, and
3. The devil's voice trying to catch you by surprise.

You must learn to distinguish each one of these three murmuring voices clearly, if you hope to adopt the correct attitude toward each one.

> Your inner voice is a special case. All of us, especially believers, must learn to control and take authority over it. Controlling your inner voice is of the utmost importance because it should be serving as your true voice and thinking and declaring only what is inside you and what you desire and order it to say.

All too often, your inner voice tends to think and say things that you do not want it to think and have not told it to say. You can learn to control your own inner voice. To do so, you must develop faith in God and lean on Him. If you lean on your faith in God, He will help you control your thoughts, banish unwanted thoughts, and eventually control your mind, which as you know, is one of the three essences of the soul and a unique human possession. Once you learn to control your own inner murmuring, you can block out and eliminate strange voices, such as the devil's voice when he comes whispering to you.

It´s been often said that you are what you eat. This may be true of the physical self, but as for your true self, your soul self, you are not what you eat. Instead, you are what you think. This, of course, applies to the natural person. At the end of the day, therefore, natural persons are what they think. Consequently, your thoughts are entirely responsible for whatever you become.

For example, the state of your PRC is determined by the types of thoughts that dominate you (your mind), the types of feelings or desires you have (your emotions), and the intentions of your heart (your will). These things determine whether the PRC remains open, half-shut, or fully blocked from God's communication.

Finally, it is important to clarify that these assertions to the effect that you are what you think refer exclusively to the natural person; that is, the person who is spiritually dead and whose heart is not indwelt by the Spirit of God. Once a person accepts and receives Jesus as his Lord and Savior, that person is born of the Spirit of God. Therefore, he or she becomes the essence of God. Such people set aside all their previous conditions and conform to the

Spirit of God. This condition takes dominion over all the others. John 3:6 says it like this:

> Flesh gives birth to flesh, but the **Spirit gives birth to spirit**. (John 3:6).

7.1. The Location of the Human Heart

When we speak of the human heart, we nearly always think of that astonishing physical organ that is located inside the thorax on the left side. Indeed, that is where this greatly admired physical organ lies. This, however, is not the spiritual heart that the Lord speaks of—the one He deeply desires you to surrender to Him. That is not the place that God so values, where His Holy Spirit dwells with every believer.

Many experts and knowers of the Word of God say that the spiritual human heart is located more or less in the lower-left section of the abdomen. However, your spiritual human heart is located in your head. Yes, the human head is the seat of the spiritual heart.

Matthew 15:19 and Mark 2:6–8, describe thoughts as coming from the heart.

> **For out of the heart come evil thoughts**—murder, adultery, sexual immorality, theft, false testimony, slander. (Matthew 15:19).

> Now some teachers of the law were sitting there, **thinking to themselves**: "Why does this fellow talk like that? He's blaspheming! Who can forgive sins but God alone?" Immediately Jesus knew in his spirit that this was what they were thinking in their hearts, and he said to them, "**Why are you thinking these things**?" (Mark 2:6–8).

Now, there's no doubt that the human mind is in the brain and the mind, emotions, and will are components of the human soul. Likewise, it's been said that when the Spirit of God comes to dwell inside your heart, He merges into your soul in a relationship of co-inherency or cohabitation. Your soul dwells in the Spirit of God, which in turn, dwells in your soul, in an indissoluble union. Through His Holy Spirit, this union enables the Lord to converts your soul into the essence of God.

In the same way, we saw above that the three components of the soul—mind, emotions, and will—exist in co-inherency with each other, which means that they are inextricably bound together. Wherever the mind is, there also are the emotions, will, and consequently, the soul. Therefore, the soul, which is your true self, is located physically inside your head. We already established that your soul is in your heart, so the natural conclusion is that the heart is located inside your head.

The Bible also says that when Moses descended from Mount Sinai after being in the presence of Jehovah, his face shone so brightly that he needed to cover his head with a veil when he was in the presence of the Israelites. This intense glow was coming from his head and more specifically, his face.

His lengthy stay in the presence of the Lord—forty days and forty nights—caused God's glory to invade his heart and soul (mind, emotions, and will). Throughout that long time with God, Moses's heart entered into fellowship with God's heart. The glow on his face was the physical reflection of God's glory in the heart of Moses, as the result of fellowship between the two hearts. As Moses spent this lengthy period before the Lord, his heart filled with the glory of God. God's Holy Spirit was not in Moses's heart but over it. Therefore, the intense brilliance of God's light focused on his heart and imprinted the intensity of His light on Moses's face.

Today when believers enter into the presence of God and spend time in fellowship with Him, their hearts enter into fellowship with God's heart. Today's believers, however, do not have to climb up a mountain the way Moses did in order to encounter God because we have the Holy Spirit of God dwelling within our very hearts. As a believer, all you need to do is call on His holy name enter into fellowship with Him and be filled with God's Spirit.

As you spend more time in His presence, the fellowship between your two hearts will grow ever deeper. Today, things are different from the way things happened to Moses, whose heart entered into fellowship with God's heart through His Holy Spirit, which was located outside of Moses, illuminated him, and shone from outside him. The difference is that today's believers have the Holy Spirit dwelling in their hearts. When we enter into fellowship with God's Spirit, the relationship comes from inside.

Therefore, as believers our faces appear peaceful, beautiful, angelic, and yes, with a certain glow or shining of light. However, they do not have the same intensity as the glowing face of Moses, who was exposed for a long period to God's light, which came from outside of Moses. A clear difference between the two cases is that Moses's light was a reflection of God´s light while our lights is not reflected, but comes from within because the light is in us, the Holy Spirit of God is in us, and our new natures as believers are ones of light.

7.2. Qualities of the Human Heart

The human heart is the epicenter of our spiritual life. It is the place where God dwells with us. The supra conscious is located within the human heart. That is where our thoughts take place. Proverbs 6:18 lists six things that the Lord hates and seven that are detestable to Him, one of which is

> **[A] heart that devises wicked schemes,** feet that are quick to rush into evil, (Proverbs 6:18).

The human soul is located in the heart. The spiritual mouth is located in the heart as well, and indeed, it is through the mouth that you express your heart's thoughts. Your physical mouth is nothing but an organ that speaks out your thoughts in the natural world so that they can be perceived through the hearing of people´s natural senses.

Your human heart is also, the repository or storage place of all your thoughts, emotions, and expressions of will, your whole life long, both the good and the evil—they are all stored there.

With the heart, you hear spiritually. In the heart, your supra senses are located, which are your spiritual senses. Your heart is where life exists. Proverbs 4:23 states it clearly:

> Above all else, **guard your heart, for everything you do flows from it**. (Proverbs 4:23).

For all these reasons, you need to jealously guard your heart, because ultimately and in essence, what is in your heart is what defines you as human being.

7.2.1. The Heart Is a Powerful Processor with a Robust Hard Drive

We have seen that the human heart is where all thoughts take place and that it is the repository and storehouse of all thoughts, emotions, and expressions of the will. It has other functions as well, one of which is to serve as a powerful processor, similar to that of a computer's hard drive.

However, while the hard drive on your computer is easily wiped clean, you do not have the capacity on your own to cleanse your heart of either good or evil thoughts. Only God can wipe clean the human heart. This cleansing can occur only when the Holy Spirit enters into the human heart and takes up His dwelling there. Proverbs 20:9 very clearly shows that it is impossible for human beings to cleanse their own hearts.

> **Who can say, "I have kept my heart pure**; I am clean and without sin"? (Proverbs 20:9).

If God does not cleanse your heart, it will hold onto all your thoughts, emotions, and expressions of the will, both good and evil, and keep them in reserve your whole life long. It is a sort of hard drive, and only God can reformat it. There is a significant difference, though. When you reformat the hard drive on your computer, it loses all its information, but God's reformat of the human heart is selective. It only removes the evil, the bad thoughts, and the negative emotions that contaminate the heart. When God reformats the human heart, everything that pleases Him remains intact.

7.2.2. The Heart and Its Infinite Infrastructure

As was said before, when God created humans, He conditioned their hearts and endowed them with the infinite infrastructure that they would need for the Spirit of God to dwell within them. Indeed, what God did was prepare His people as the potential temple of God. For this purpose, He created in their hearts a throne where He could rule over their lives.

You can either become a temple of God or choose not to. The decision is entirely yours. It is the result of your own choice and the exercise of your free will.

Remember that when Adam and Eve sinned and God's Spirit departed from their hearts, God left behind the infinite infrastructure. He did not remove His throne from the human heart.

Therefore, all human beings, without exception, hold an infinite infrastructure within their hearts. This coupling station possesses all the divine, infinite conditions that are necessary to house the Holy Spirit. This way, when the spiritual conditions are right, God can return to dwell in each heart. Thus, when God withdrew from the human heart, He left behind an empty throne in the infinite infrastructure or the coupling station, and only God can come back to occupy that empty throne.

Therefore, the infinite infrastructure is what makes it possible for the Spirit of God to enter in and dwell with His people. It is also, what facilitates communication with them, by means of the PRC, which we discussed earlier.

In summary, when Adam and Eve sinned, they died because the Spirit of God uncoupled from the coupling station and pulled out of their hearts. He took from them the image and likeness of God, and they were left separate from Him. However, the Lord did leave behind the coupling station or the infinite infrastructure that God had installed when He had created them. He withdrew His Holy Spirit but left behind the empty throne of God. This is because God never gave up on us.

Instead, He held onto His people as a fundamental part of His plan to fulfill His purpose—to form His family and have a lineage. He knew that if He did not give up on us, that infinite infrastructure, coupling station, or empty throne would be essential for carrying out phase two of His plan. Phase 2 was when He would make His Son, Jesus Christ, a mediator between Gods and people so that the Spirit of God would once again dwell with them. This would only be possible if their hearts met all the conditions that were necessary. The coupling station or throne of God would stay behind, making it possible for the everlasting God to once again indwell and reign in the human heart, transforming His people back to His image and into the likeness of God.

7.3. God and the Hologram Principle

By the dogma of their faith, believers know and accept that there is just one God and that He is omnipresent. Therefore, He is fully and simultaneously present in the three persons of the Holy Trinity—Father, Son, and Holy Spirit. Believers also accept the fact that this same God, by means of the Holy Spirit, also dwells fully and simultaneously in the heart of each believer. Unquestionably, this has been a hidden mystery and has tickled the curiosity of most believers, who, by faith, have accepted it as dogma. They are convinced that nothing is impossible for God.

God is revealing an explanation of His dispensation's mystery concerning the three persons of the Holy Trinity and His presence in the hearts of millions of believers—past, present, and future. It is by means of the Hologram Principle that God distributes and deposits himself in every one of those hearts simultaneously, without losing His wholeness. To understand the full dimension of this wonder, we need to know what a hologram is and understand its main features.

7.3.1. What Is a Hologram?

A hologram is a three-dimensional photograph of an object taken with the help of a laser beam. A hologram is made by projecting the light from a laser onto the object to be photographed. A second laser beam is then, projected onto the light that is reflected from the first one. The resulting interference pattern—the area where the two intersect—is caught on film.

When the film is developed, it looks like an insignificant spiral of light with dark lines. If a third laser beam is then, trained on the developed film, a three-dimensional image of the original object comes into view. The astonishing result of this process is not the three-dimensional image that appears but what happens next. When the hologram of any object—for example, a flower —is split into equal halves, if targeted by a laser beam, either half will contain the complete image of the original object, in this case, the flower.

If the two halves are divided again, each scrap of film will contain a smaller but full, complete, and intact version of the original object's image. Holograms are very different from conventional photographs because each piece contains all the information of the whole. This quality of the hologram—the whole in its parts—breaks old paradigms and gives us an entirely new way of understanding the organization and order of things.

The interesting twist in all this is that historically, Western science and culture have held the thesis that any physical phenomenon; can be best understood by analyzing its parts. A hologram teaches us that this thesis does not apply to certain phenomena in the universe. If we try to break up something that was constructed holographically, we cannot separate it into parts for analysis because when we divide it, all we get is a smaller version of the same thing. Thus, the Hologram Principle states that when a hologram is broken up, each of its parts contains its totality. In other words, the whole is in the parts.

7.3.2. Application of the Hologram Principle

When God created Adam in His image and likeness, what He really did was deposit His Holy Spirit in Adam's heart. He divided himself as a sort of super hologram and placed this piece of himself into Adam's heart. Following the same Hologram Principle, this means that the Spirit of God dwelt fully and wholly inside Adam's heart.

God uses this Hologram Principle to be present simultaneously, in all His fullness, in His three persons: Father, Son, and Holy Spirit. Each one is as a piece of the super hologram of God because each one of the three persons retains, fully and wholly, the divine features of God.

By the same Hologram Principle, God, through His Holy Spirit, dispenses or deposits himself in all believers and dwells simultaneously in all His fullness in the heart of every one of His sons and daughters. This is very important because it allows the Lord to be a very personal and special God in the life of every believer.

Therefore, God created human beings, Adam and Eve, according to the Hologram Principle. He created them in His own image and likeness. Genesis 1:27 describes it as follows:

> **So God created mankind in his own image, in the image of God he created them**; male and female he created them. (Genesis 1:27).

Thinking in the natural, many people believe this image to be physical, when in fact, God has no physical image. This is the spiritual image of God, the essence of God.

When God created Adam and Eve, He blessed them and ordered them to multiply, be fruitful, and fill the earth. It was His will for the earth to be filled with His children, all made in His image and likeness. God's plan was to multiply himself in His people, following the Hologram Principle.

God placed much of the success of His plan in human hands, though, and since He also gave them free will, the fall of Adam and Eve pushed Him into phase two of His plan. Thus, when His people fell into disobedience, they ceased to be of the image and likeness of God and lost the Spirit of God.

The image of God is like a piece of God's hologram inserted into the hearts of Adam and Eve. He created them by dwelling inside them through His Holy Spirit, applying the Hologram Principle.

God's will was that Adam and Eve and all their offspring live forever. That is why he instructed them very clearly about what was allowed and what was forbidden in the Garden of Eden. Him. Genesis 2:16–17 says,

> And the Lord God commanded the man, "You are free to eat from any tree in the garden; **but you must not eat from the tree of the knowledge of good and evil**, for when you eat from it you will certainly die." (Genesis 2:16-17).

Therefore, it was their disobedience that produced their fall. In turn, this introduced death among human beings.

It also needs to be stressed, that when God gave life to Eve from Adam's rib, He actually separated out and took a piece of God's hologram that was in Adam (his Holy Spirit) and so breathe life into Eve. This way, Eve was also made in the image and likeness of God because the Lord inserted His Holy Spirit (the piece of God's hologram), into her heart. Thus, the fullness of God came to dwell within both their hearts. Before they disobeyed and fell, they had the full divine essence because the Holy Spirit lived in their hearts.

7.4. The Corruption of the Human Heart

After the fall of Adam and Eve, the human life span, still extended to several hundred years. The reason is that when the fall had only just happened, they retained relative proximity to their original spiritual condition, which was alongside their new physical condition. It was a sort of remnant of the spiritual life that they had left behind after the fall. Also, the PRC of their supra conscious was still open, which preserved their flow of life or instinct of self-preservation and kept it relatively strong. In relative terms, they were still comparatively more spiritual than physical beings. The fullness of evil had not yet taken complete dominion over the human heart.

As the years went by and decades became centuries, their natural selves took stronger hold and the human being became more physical and less spiritual. As a result, the intensity of the PRC began to weaken, and along with it, the human instinct for self-preservation. In short, God created His people (Adam and Eve) righteous and perfect, but they strayed from the path. King Solomon says as much in Ecclesiastes 7:29.

> This only have I found: **God created mankind upright, but they have gone in search of many schemes**. (Ecclesiastes 7:29).

Evil increasingly corrupted the human heart and separated God from His people. As they multiplied, their evilness grew. This is clear in Genesis 6:5.

> **The Lord saw how great the wickedness of the human race had become on the earth**, and that every inclination of the thoughts of the human heart was only evil all the time. (Genesis 6:5).

The people drifted farther and farther away from their creator. As a result, they left behind their eternal nature, which had been the original condition of Adam and Eve, and took on a new status. At first, they lived many hundreds of years, but their life expectancy began to decline until they finally reached their current state, in which the Lord set an average human life span of seventy years.

When they separated from God, their hearts were corrupted, they lost their righteousness and perfection, and were consumed with every kind of evil. With the passage of time, sin continued to atrophy their spiritual senses and build up their natural senses. The result was that they forgot and abandoned their Creator and began to worship creation in His place. Let's look at 2nd Kings 17:16.

> They forsook all the commands of the Lord their God and made for themselves two idols cast in the shape of calves, and an Asherah pole. **They bowed down to all the starry hosts, and they worshiped Baal**. (2nd. Kings 17:16).

7.4.1. The Natural Person Is Not the Image and Likeness of God

There is a widespread, untrue belief that we are all born in the image and likeness of God. The actual truth is that man and woman were created in the image and likeness of God, which is not the same thing. God did indeed create them in His image and after His likeness. However, as we have seen, after the fall of Adam and Eve, they lost their image and likeness of God and ceased to be spiritual.

People were bereft of the image and likeness of God, and as of that moment, every person would forever be born natural and come into the world spiritually dead. This is why we are not born in the image and likeness of God. We are born without the Holy Spirit dwelling in our hearts, without the piece of God's hologram. Remember, the image and likeness of God, were given by the Spirit of God, who lived within the human heart. This is why the future of any newborn child will be marked, or conditioned by two mutually exclusive paths or options:

- One pathway leads us to be spirit, a condition that we can only achieve when the Spirit of God lives within our hearts. More specifically, this is when the Holy Spirit begins to cohabit or dwell with the human soul and transform it into the essence of God.
- The other pathway leads a person to continue being dust, a natural being, and part of the universe because the soul is plunged into darkness, and the person is spiritually dead.

So long, the Spirit of God does not transform the human soul, it remains in darkness and shadow, and the person remains in his or her natural state. In this natural state, we are nothing but dust. King David makes it clear in Psalms 103:14.

> For [God] knows how we are formed, **he remembers that we are dust**. (Psalms 103:14).

In our spiritually dead condition, we are far from having the image and likeness of God. Further evidence that human creatures ceased to be the image and likeness of God during the period that spans from the fall of Adam and Eve until the death and resurrection of Jesus Christ is the following declaration by King David in Psalms 17:15:

As for me, I will be vindicated and will see your face; **when I awake, I will be satisfied with seeing your likeness**. (Psalms 17:15).

Not even King David himself, that great servant of God, had the image and likeness of God. Instead, after the fall of Adam and Eve, people became strangers to God, unknown aliens. Even so, with the death and resurrection of Jesus Christ, God extended the possibility for His people to cease being aliens and strangers, and become His own children and an integral part of His sacred family, part of God's lineage.

Even the great King David was aware of his status as an alien and stranger to God and knew that he was foreign to the spiritual life because he did not have eternal life. We can read his words in 1st. Chronicles 29:15 and Psalms 39:12.

We are foreigners and strangers in your sight, as were all our ancestors. Our days on earth are like a shadow, without hope. (1st. Chronicles 29:15).

Hear my prayer, Lord, listen to my cry for help; do not be deaf to my weeping. **I dwell with you as a foreigner, a stranger, as all my ancestors were**. (Psalms 39:12).

As it happens, what we usually call life, the thing that causes us to breathe and have bodily functions is the breath or puff of life. It allows us to remain in this world. The breath of life is something that all God's creatures have—even plants and animals. Psalms 104:29 gives a clear picture of the human condition before God, as follows:

> When you hide your face, they are terrified; **when you take away their breath**, they die and return to the dust. (Psalms 104:29).

It is important recognized that human beings have the capacity to regain God's image and bear His likeness. We do this by confessing Jesus Christ as our Lord and Savior and inviting Him to dwell in our hearts. This surrender allows the Holy Spirit to enter the human heart, and this is how people can recover their piece of God's hologram. The human soul cohabiting with the Spirit of God is the piece of God's hologram, and causes the person to be born into life, taking on the image and likeness of God.

Thus, when natural men and women use their free wills to receive Jesus Christ as Lord and Savior, light or fire immediately issues forth from the kingdom of God and illumines their hearts, where it then deposits the Holy Spirit (the piece of God's hologram). This is how God redeems His people from death, revives them, and gives them life. This is when the Holy Spirit begins to dwell with them, inside their hearts.

Once the Holy Spirit enters your heart, you are born again with two natures:

1. The nature of God, your Father, and
2. The nature of the bride of the Lamb, your mother.

A new creature comes to life, born of a Father (Almighty God) and a mother (the bride of the Lamb or the church).

Both natures and essences are spiritual. Remember that God created man and woman with a spiritual essence that was different from His own. This essence is the human soul. As a result, the bride of the Lamb, the sum and composite of all the redeemed, transformed, and revived souls of believers, becomes a sort of super soul. At the same time, it is the church, the mother of all the children of God. This completes the perfect concept of the family—father, mother, and children—who are the outcome of both spiritual essences. Just as the natural person's lineage is the outcome of the carnal or physical essence of the father and mother, even so, the lineage of God is the product of the spiritual essence of the Father (God the father) and mother (the bride of the Lamb), which is the church.

When believers depart from this world, the piece of God's hologram, the Holy Spirit, returns to God, taking with Him the believer's soul. The Spirit of God becomes a companion to the human soul. This union between the Spirit of God and the human soul is an indissoluble unit (the child of God). This redeemed, transformed, and revived soul is simultaneously a precious, living stone, which gradually combines with other precious, living stones (other redeemed, transformed, and revived souls). They are being built and being formed into the church of Christ, the new dwelling place of God, the body of Christ, the bride of the Lamb, and the mother of all believers and children of God. Later, we will see that this is also the New Jerusalem.

To corroborate the fact that the body of Christ (the church) is also God´s dwelling place and His holy temple, let´s look at Ephesians 2:19–22.

> Consequently, you are no longer foreigners and strangers, but fellow citizens with God's people, and also members of his household, built on the foundation of the apostles and prophets, with Christ Jesus himself as the chief cornerstone. In him the whole building is joined together and rises to become **a holy temple in the Lord**. And in him you too are being built together **to become a dwelling in which God lives by his Spirit**. (Ephesians 2:19-22).

In summary, when you accept Jesus Christ into your heart, the Holy Spirit inoculates your soul. Your soul acquires the essence of God so that life is born and you become a child of God. The Spirit of God merges inextricably with your soul, it changes your natural essence into the Lord's spiritual essence, and you acquire the image and likeness of God.

7.5. The Inverse Hologram Principle

We have already seen how God, by the Hologram Principle and through His Holy Spirit, distributes and pours himself fully into millions of believers' hearts and dwells simultaneously with each, and every one of them, even as He continues to be the one and only one.

The bride of Christ, which in turn is God's new dwelling place, is being built up through the addition and integration of redeemed, transformed, and revived souls of millions of believers, from all eras of human history and from all over the world. Thus, the bride of the Lamb is being built, into a type of super soul, revived by the Spirit of God. This is possible through the Inverse Hologram Principle.

The souls of the many saved people are been melded into a single overriding soul, which will be transformed into the bride of the Lamb. At the same time, the soul of each believer, that is united, in co-inherency or cohabitation with the Holy Spirit, will maintain its wholeness and individuality, so much so, that every saved person will also be a child of God. This is clear in Romans 12:5.

> So in Christ we, **though many, form one body**, and each member belongs to all the others. (Romans 12:5).

God uses the Hologram Principle and the Inverse Hologram Principle to carry out His eternal purpose of founding His family and establishing His lineage. All this happens while at the same time, He is building His holy temple or dwelling place.

Therefore, just as God, by the Hologram Principle, continues to divide, distribute, and simultaneously pours himself out into the heart of each, and every believer, while never losing His wholeness nor singleness. Meanwhile, by means of the Inverse Hologram Principle, He is also bringing together all the redeemed, transformed, and revived souls of the believers into a single soul. A single, great, and revived soul that will be the bride of the Lamb while at the same time, the soul of every believer, in inextricable union with the Holy Spirit, will maintain its individual existence as a son or daughter of God. The Lord Jesus Christ himself describes the eternal union between the Spirit of God and the human soul in John 14:16, when He says,

> "And I will ask the Father, and he will give you another advocate, **to help you and be with you forever**". (John 14:16).

Both principles were, applied in Jesus Christ for the first time (the Hologram Principle and Inverse Hologram Principle). In John 16:28, Jesus Christ says it this way:

> **I came from the Father and entered the world; now I am leaving the world and going back to the Father**. (John 16:28).

In summary, God is the one and only. By the Hologram Principle, He distributes himself among many while continuing to be the one. By the Inverse Hologram Principle, God gathers many souls into a single soul (the bride of the Lamb) while they continue to be many.

A very important conclusion is that God possesses many traits, among them, is being a super hologram. And His plan is for the bride of the Lamb to have also, the characteristics of a mirroring super hologram, a sort of super-revived soul that consists of the integration of all the redeemed, transformed, and revived souls of all the believers of all times since the death and resurrection of Jesus Christ.

Chapter 8

FROM PHASE ONE TO PHASE TWO OF GOD'S PLAN

Phase one of God's plan was to build His lineage on the foundation of men and women who would obey Him in holiness, exercise their free wills, and agree to become part of His family. Obedience to God, still today as it was yesterday, has always been the sine qua non, the necessary and indispensable condition for people to remain in holiness and thereby, become part of God's family and have a place in His lineage. Most of all, God expects them to obey Him. Although as explained early on, His people made use of their free will and chose to disobey Him.

When they disobeyed God in the phase one of His plan, He initiated a second phase of the same plan. It was all part of His unshaken intention to found His family and give himself a lineage, which was His heart's deep desire. Phase one stumbled, due entirely to the actions of the people and not to God. However, it did not change God's purpose, which was, and still is the same—to found His family and establish His new dwelling place.

God entrusted the success of phase one of His plan into His people's hands. They did not rise to His expectations. The Lord then moved into phase two, sending His Son, Jesus, to lift up the people and thus safeguard and guarantee the success of God's eternal plan this time around. It was the final and definitive phase, because there will never be a phase three.

God's decision was so unyielding that in order to carry out phase two of His purposes' fulfillments; He made the drastic decision to send His Own Son to be sacrificed. He made sure that this time, it would be a resounding success. Therefore, He did not leave the building of His family entirely in human hands. The phase two of God's plan was to send His Only Son to be sacrificed and to redeem His people from the hands of death, which had taken dominion over them from the time that Adam and Eve had fallen. In this way, God hoped to deliver His people from their growing corruption and the hardening of their hearts so that they could make a U-turn and walk down a new path of obedience. They would finally take the road of life that God offered to those who would become part of His family.

8.1. The Essential Differences between Phase One and Phase Two of God's Plan

These are essentially the same differences that existed between the first Adam and the last Adam, between Adam and Jesus Christ. As we know, God launched phase one by creating a man and a woman and causing His Holy Spirit to dwell in their hearts and fashion them in His own image and likeness. When they disobeyed him, God departed from them and left them to die spiritually. They moved from life into death, from freedom into bondage, and they became slaves to sin.

Phase 2 begins when people are born already separated from God, spiritually dead, and without the image and likeness of God. However, when they accept Jesus Christ as their Lord and Savior, the Spirit of God enters their hearts and dwells with them. They step from death into life, form bondage into freedom, and once again, they take on the image and likeness of God.

Phase one, then, was founded on the first Adam, whose disobedience and failure brought death to all humankind, while phase two, was built on Jesus Christ, the last Adam, whose obedience and success brought life to all.

God's phase two essentially reversed the whole process of phase one. Nevertheless, it is important to understand that both phases share a key requirement: Each person must exercise their free will to either choose or reject God's offer to join His family.

In short, with the launch of phase one, God put much of the responsibility of forming His family into human hands. Adam and Eve were given instructions to love God and obey Him in everything, which meant being fruitful, multiplying, and filling the earth so that their descendants would also be righteous and perfect. They would have the Spirit of God dwelling in and with them. The piece of God's hologram would be in their hearts. Consequently, they would have the image and likeness of God as well.

The above is the human lineage, the children that God would inherit to build His family; they would be the living, precious stones that God could use to build His dwelling place. We all know that those first people failed. They were unable to remain faithful to their Lord and Creator, so God needed to move into phase two of His plan by sending His Son to reach out His hand to them. This time, God made sure, through His Son, that He could eliminate every possibility of failure and that His people would be successful and victorious, enabling God to build the family that He so desire.

It is worth noting that from the fall of Adam and Eve until the arrival of Jesus Christ (the last Adam), men and women had not known the privilege of having God dwelling with them in their hearts. Abraham, Moses, David, Esther, and Deborah (to name just a few of God's most prominent servants) did not have such privilege. During that time, all human beings lived in sin, they had no Spirit of God dwelling with them, and their hearts lacked the piece of God's hologram.

It was not until after the death and resurrection of Jesus Christ—when He redeemed them from sin and death—that God resumed the process of reintroducing His Holy Spirit to the human heart. Only then was the Lord able to deposit or pour out the piece of God's hologram into their hearts, transforming them back into the image and likeness of God.

8.2. Jesus Is the Temple of the Holy Spirit

Jesus Christ is the only human being who was not born spiritually dead because He came into the world with the Spirit of God already incorporated into Him and dwelling with Him in His heart. When He was born, He came into the world already as a temple of the Holy Spirit (much as Adam and Eve did at creation) because the fullness of God, through His Holy Spirit, dwelt with and in Him from birth.

8.3. Human Beings Make a U-Turn

As was said, after the fall of Adam and Eve, people had essentially been traveling down the path of death and moving farther and farther away from God. It was not until after the death and resurrection of Jesus Christ that humanity made a U-turn on the road of life because Jesus opened the way. God gave life to the dead by cleansing and redeeming them from death through the blood of Jesus Christ and restoring His Holy Spirit in their hearts.

8.4. The Destiny of the Righteous Ones, Who Fell Asleep before the Death and Resurrection of Jesus Christ

Before the death and resurrection of Jesus Christ, not even the righteous, upon leaving this world, could go to heaven or the bosom of God. No matter how righteous they may have been, they held the corrupt, sinful human condition, and did not have the piece of God's hologram (the Holy Spirit) in their hearts. The Holy Spirit serves as a kind of admission ticket or passport, without which, no one can enter the kingdom of God. Faced with all this, God decided to prepare a temporary home where the righteous could stay. They were separate from Him as they awaited the coming of Jesus, who would eventually bring their admission ticket or passport and open the way for them to enter into God's presence.

8.4.1. Paradise

All the righteous ones who fell asleep before the death and resurrection of Jesus Christ, such as Abraham, Job, Moses, Ruth, Deborah, David, and Esther, were in a temporary dwelling called Paradise or the bosom of

Abraham. Because they were righteous or holy, they could be sheltered and set apart for God. Their final destination would be Heaven, also called God's dwelling place, the temple of God, the city of God, the holy city, or the New Jerusalem. At the time they departed this world, as we have seen, they could not enter into Heaven, because the Spirit of God was not in them and their souls did not have the ticket or traveling companion who would take them directly into God's arms. They did not have the piece of God's hologram that brings about the process of reunification with God when He takes the human soul to himself. The truth is that after the fall of Adam and Eve and up until the coming of Jesus Christ, no person had the admission ticket to God's presence.

God therefore, created Paradise to house all those righteous souls who lived after the fall of Adam and Eve and before the arrival, death, and resurrection of Jesus Christ. It was after the death and resurrection of Jesus Christ that the kingdom of God was thrown, open and, all those who were in Paradise, rose again and were, revived by the same Spirit that breathed life back into Jesus Christ, and after they received their piece of God's hologram, they were able to enter Heaven. At last, Paradise said farewell to its illustrious guests and was closed forever.

8.4.2. Another Paradise in an Exalted Place Not on Earth

We have seen that Paradise, or the bosom of Abraham, was the holding place for all God´s servants that had fallen asleep or departed this world before the arrival, death, and resurrection of Jesus Christ. We need to understand that there is another Paradise—a mini paradise - that is on high but separate from God and where Enoch and Elijah dwell. They are the only servants of God who did not experience physical death on Earth. Instead, both were taken up by God and held in a mini paradise, which God had set in place to receive and shelter them while they awaited the time to fulfill the mission for which they´ve been taken up. Therefore, they are being held, aside to receive their admission ticket, which is the Holy Spirit or their piece of God's hologram. We now know that this is an essential requirement for anyone to enter Heaven, God's Kingdom.

Over the ages, many questions have been asked in relation to the whereabouts of Enoch and Elijah. Let´s look at what the scripture says in Genesis 5:22–24 and 2nd. Kings 2:11, concerning the way these two God´s servants, were taken out of this world.

> After he became the father of Methuselah, Enoch walked faithfully with God 300 years and had other sons and daughters. Altogether, Enoch lived

> a total of 365 years. Enoch walked faithfully with God; **then he was no more, because God took him away**. (Genesis 5:22–24).

Elijah's departure took place while he was still with his disciple Elisha, who had asked him for a double portion of his spirit.

> As they were walking along and talking together, suddenly a chariot of fire and horses of fire appeared and separated the two of them, **and Elijah went up to heaven in a whirlwind**. (2nd. Kings 2:11).

Some people confuse these two cases with the fate of Moses who wasn't taken nor was swept up by God, but rather, at God's order, he climbed the mountain and died there, on Earth. A dispute over Moses's body even broke out between the archangel Michael and the devil, as we see in Jude 9.

> **But even the archangel Michael, when he was disputing with the devil about the body of Moses**, did not himself dare to condemn him for slander but said, "The Lord rebuke you!". (Jude 9).

It should be clear, then, that Moses wasn't swept up nor taken by God as Enoch and Elijah had been. After his death on the mountain, he was in the bosom of Abraham, like all the other righteous ones who left this world before the death and resurrection of Jesus Christ. The only two exceptions were Enoch and Elijah.

Even though, these men were both taken up by the Lord himself; under no circumstance they are with Him because they still lacked their admission ticket or passport, the Holy Spirit, the piece of God's hologram, which as we have discussed earlier, is the essential requirement for any human being to enter the kingdom of God.

Jesus Christ clearly confirmed this requirement in John 14:6 to answer a question from Thomas. Thomas asked Him how they could know the way if they did not know where He was going.

> Jesus answered, I am the way and the truth and the life. **No one comes to the Father except through me**. (John 14:6).

It should be perfectly clear that without Jesus, who is the Way, no one can go to the Father; that is, into the kingdom of God. Although, Enoch and Elijah were taken up by God himself. Even after all these years, they still have not gone to the Father.

8.4.3. When and How Will Enoch and Elijah Receive Their Tickets to Enter into the Arms of God?

Many have asked how Enoch and Elijah will enter into the Holy of Holies - the Arms of God - if they left this world without having received the Spirit of God in their hearts, which is the essential or indispensable condition for entering into the everlasting presence of God. We can examine several truths to find the answer, which has been shadowed in mystery for a long time.

1. Without exception, no one can enter into the presence of God without an admission ticket or passport, which is the Holy Spirit, the piece of God's hologram. Only those who´s souls have been redeemed, transformed, and revived by the Spirit of God can enter into the Holy of Holies in the presence of God.
2. The ticket, which is the Holy Spirit, the piece of God's hologram can only be delivered, and be received in this world, to which the Lord sent the Comforter for all humankind. No one can receive it elsewhere.
3. Everyone, including the great servants of God, were stained by the stigma of death that was brought by original sin. This means that they could be cleansed and redeemed only by the blood of the Lamb that

was slain which was the only blood able to clean this stain and stigma forever so that all people could see God face-to-face.

If all these facts; are settled beyond doubt, how will God untie this knot and finally be able to enjoy the presence of His beloved servants Enoch and Elijah? Remember they had been already, taken up from the world, and therefore, they were not in the bosom of Abraham. Consequently, they could not rise again together with all God's servants, as Job, Abraham, Ruth, Samuel, Esther, and so many others had done, when they received their admission ticket or passport at the dramatic moment when the Lord Jesus Christ completed His mission, by taking onto His own shoulders the sin of all humanity. Then He began to hand out tickets for people to attain eternal life.

The Lord is still handing out tickets today. It is clear that Enoch and Elijah were not included in the handouts. They still have no admission tickets to the presence of God, which means, they are still waiting for their turns, as they remain in the mini paradise where they were placed.

The question, then, still stands: How will God get Enoch and Elijah their tickets, if these are handed out only in this world and they are no longer here? Could the Lord have set aside Enoch and Elijah for some specific mission? Does He intend to bring them back into this world and then seize the moment of their mission so that while they are here, they can receive their admission ticket or passport and He can then take them into His presence? The answer is a resounding, "Yes." God has Enoch and Elijah standing ready for their mission to be the two witnesses that He introduces in Revelation 11. They are the same two witnesses that many believers have split into warring camps over, disputing about who they are and where they will come from. The answer is that they are none other than Enoch and Elijah, who will finally emerge from their mini paradise to fulfill the mission that the Lord has been holding them for and for which, they were removed from the world without experiencing conventional death.

Let´s take a look at what the Lord says about the two witnesses through the apostle John in Revelation 11:3–5.

> And I will appoint my two witnesses, and they will prophesy for 1,260 days, clothed in sackcloth." They are "the two olive trees" and the two lampstands, and "they stand before the Lord of the earth." If anyone tries to harm them, fire comes from their mouths and devours their enemies. This is how anyone who wants to harm them must die. (Revelation 11:3-5).

These two witnesses of God, Enoch and Elijah, will thus come with great power, to be witnesses and prophets of God for three and a half years. After that time, God will allow them to be overcome and killed by the devil. Three and a half days after they have been dumped into the public square of the city, the Lord will revive them. Then and only then, Enoch and Elijah will receive their admission ticket—the Spirit of God or their piece of God's hologram. After that, they will be swept up once again. This time, it is not to a temporary holding place but to fall into God's arms for all eternity. Look at Revelation 11:11–12.

> But after the three and a half days **the breath of life [the Holy Spirit] from God entered them**, and they stood on their feet, and terror struck those who saw them. Then they heard a loud voice from heaven saying to them, "Come up here." **And they went up to heaven in a cloud**, while their enemies looked on. (Revelation 11: 11-12).

Thus, God's two witnesses will be Enoch and Elijah, who are still in a mini paradise somewhere above and are waiting to carry out the mission for which God caught them up. In the process, they will receive their admission tickets, which will allow them to be redeemed, transformed, and revived by the same Spirit who revived Jesus Christ, and ultimately, they will be united with the Lord in His kingdom.

8.5. Human Beings: Are They Precious Living Stones or Scaffolding?

As we saw earlier, nothing and no one can escape God's sovereign will. Everything, and everybody, without exception, fits into the framework of His purposes. Neither sinners, criminals, nor traitors can escape His will, but instead, they are part of it.

So what is the difference between those who accept the offer to become part of God's family and those who decline it? The difference is that those who agree to join God's family will be become living, precious stones, which will be fitted into His family. They will be part of His holy dwelling place for all eternity. Meanwhile, those who decline God's offer will be part of the scaffolding used to build and fulfill His eternal purposes of establishing His royal family, namely, His holy dwelling place. As we all know, once a construction is complete, scaffoldings are torn down and discarded. Therefore, everyone will have contributed to God's plans and purposes, without exception.

As God carries out His purpose, He will even make use of the evil that is lurking in human hearts. This does not mean that these people are somehow relieved of responsibility for their faults and the sins that they have committed. The scriptures are filled with such cases. It is enough to recall the story of Judas Iscariot. His treachery did not become less of sin just because God used it to fulfill His plan of salvation for all humankind through Jesus Christ. The Lord speaks about this very clearly in Mark 14:21.

> The Son of Man will go just as it is written about him. **But woe to that man who betrays the Son of Man!** It would be better for him if he had not been born. (Mark 14:21).

When people use their free will to choose their destiny, their choice essentially opens up two mutually exclusive pathways:

1. They choose to become living, precious stones for building God's holy dwelling place, thus becoming part of God's family.
2. They choose to become part of the scaffoldings used to build the home, thus choosing to be discarded and locked out of God's family for all eternity.

It should be clear that regardless of the choice they make, people can't elude participation in building the Lord's project. The difference is that under the first option, they become part of God's holy dwelling place, while under the second; they are discarded and eliminated, the same way that scaffoldings are discarded at the end of all construction.

From the day of his or her birth, everyone faces the decision and will need to give a fundamental answer to the following dilemma: What do you chose to be? You choose to be a building stone or a scaffolding of the construction of God's holy temple? Whatever your answer is, you will be making full use of your free will, a freedom that is within the exclusive power of each person and in which God does not interfere, because He wants to be certain that we all exercise it freely, as free will implies.

God introduces and promotes His counteroffer, making sure that everyone has a clear view of both options. This way He can be certain that you know His desire to have you personally in His family as part of His lineage. Indeed, God is constantly giving unmistakable signs of His greatness and infinite creativity through His ingenious creation and His great love and mercy. He offers a clear path to himself. God does something else as well. He tries to woo people to win their souls. He does this by using His very essence—love. God is deeply in love with people. This love leads Him, to forgive over, and over again, and keep on forgiving our never-ending transgressions. It is what makes Him deploy His immeasurable mercy and grace on our behalves. Even so, some people remain rebellious. They do not allow themselves to be won over; even though, God yearns to have a romance with us, but all too often, some turn Him down.

The dilemma in which we inevitably find ourselves as we pass through this world is very simple but essential: We must choose to be a precious, living stone or a scaffolding in the building of God's holy dwelling place. God forever and always sets these only two choices before every human being. As we have already seen, we have complete freedom to choose and define our own destiny.

Fulfilling His own purposes and in accordance with His divine goodness, God created everyone to become a precious, living stone in His holy dwelling place. He wants us to be part of His family and to enter His lineage. The Lord did something else as well. He gave us the capacity and privilege to become producers and suppliers of more precious, living stones for the building of God's holy dwelling place. We do this via our families. This is the very reason why God created the institution of the family for himself. He set it up between men and women so that they could become fruitful, multiply, and have sons and daughters. This was God's mechanism to obtain His own sons and daughters, the precious, living stones for building His dwelling place.

God assigned couples the responsibility to raise their children in the instruction and admonition of the Lord. The purpose is to shield them from evil, keep them in holiness, and set them on a straight path to God.

Some families do produce precious, living stones that God is very pleased with, while others produce scaffolding, for which God suffers much sorrow and sadness because, in the end, they will be discarded and lost forever.

All families with children, without exception, provide building supplies for God's construction project, His holy family, that is, His dwelling place. The difference is that some families supply precious, living stones while others provide scaffolding. Of course, some believers may have lived the first part of their lives as scaffolding, but later by the grace and mercy of God, they accepted and received Jesus Christ as Lord and Savior. Therefore, they are transformed and converted into precious living stones for the construction of God's dwelling place. Where they end up is all that really matters and not necessarily their early steps.

One of the most significant cases of transformation from scaffolding into precious, living stone is the apostle Paul, whose divine conversion was spectacular, dramatic, and awe-inspiring. Even so, no one should deliberately live in sin, trusting that the opportunity will eventually arise to switch side hoping he or she will be transformed. Because before the transition is complete, death could have the last word and wrest away the opportunity to receive the Lord and undergo the transformation that is needed to enter into eternal life. Furthermore, the Lord's Second Coming could take us all by surprise and leave us with very few options for achieving salvation.

Finally, it would be remiss not to point out that every personal decision has consequences. These consequences can be critical for life or death, especially when they involve the exercise of free will in accepting or rejecting God. One man whose free will had consequences that changed the entire world was Jacob. He was the direct precursor of the people of Israel, who, while traveling to the house of his uncle Laban in Paddan Aram, freely chose the Lord as his God. It is described in Genesis 28:20–21.

> Then Jacob made a vow, saying, "If God will be with me and will watch over me on this journey I am taking and will give me food to eat and clothes to wear so that I return safely to my father's household, **then the Lord will be my God**. (Genesis 28:20-21).

A number of lessons can be drawn from this story of Jacob's very clear and unusual exercise of free will to accept the Lord as his God:

1. Although Jacob was the grandson and son of the patriarchs Abraham and Isaac, this was not enough. He had to make his own decision to accept the Lord as his God, which once again confirms that salvation is very personal.

2. Unexpectedly, Jacob set conditions on his acceptance, insisting that the Lord should watch over him, sustain him by feeding and dressing him, and return him safely to his father's house. The Lord accepted these conditions and honored them abundantly.
3. Clearly, the relationship or position that each person has with God, stemming from conversion, can be unique and personal, so long as the person practices integrity. This being the case, God generally responds to specific requests.

8.6. Two Dimensions of the Human Race's Great Mission

Humankind has a great mission on this Earth. It consists of two essential parts or dimensions. The first part is to accept the Lord's offer to join God's family. The second part is to become an effective instrument so that other people can also accept God's offer. This second part begins in your own family. Thus, the first part of every person's mission is to accept the Lord's offer to become a precious, living stone for the construction of God's new dwelling place. The second part is to become a useful instrument, to help others to become, also, precious, living stones for God's divine purpose.

By fulfilling this two-dimensional mission, you actually fulfill the two great commandments that Jesus Christ left us through His disciples. Jesus gave them the first commandment in Mark 12:29–30.

> **Love the Lord your God with all your heart and with all your soul and with all your mind and with all your strength**. The most important [commandment] is this. (Mark 12:29-30).

The love of God will lead us to obey Him and accept His offer to become part of His lineage. In doing so, we become precious, living stones. Thereby, we become part of God's family, His holy dwelling place.

Mark 12:31 gives the second great commandment.

> The second is this: **Love your neighbor as yourself**. There is no commandment greater than these. (Mark 12:31).

If you love your neighbor as yourself, that love induces you to bring your neighbor to that love so that he or she can obey and accept the offer to become another precious, living stone for building God's holy dwelling place and to join His family.

Thus, the two commandments that the Lord Jesus Christ left us through His disciples are much more practical than they appear to be at first sight. In practice, love for God and for your neighbor should propel you into accepting and receiving Jesus Christ as your Lord and Savior and striving without ceasing to help your neighbor accept Him and receive Him also as Lord and Savior.

8.6.1. So What Does It Mean to Love God?

People tend to confuse love with the attraction and feelings experienced between a man and a woman. This, however, is not true love. The attraction and feelings that a couple experiences are nearly always involuntary sensations, which people themselves do not entirely control. Indeed, they are temporary feelings. They nearly always fade and flicker out as quickly as they appeared. They do not arise from a personal decision. By contrast, true love is a personal decision, and it can only be snuffed out by someone's personal will.

So what does it mean to love God? How can we love God? The definition of loving God is submitting to him, obeying him, and keeping His Word.

In John 14:23 and John 15:10, Jesus Christ himself explains it this way:

> Jesus replied, "**Anyone who loves me will obey my teaching**. My Father will love them, and we will come to them and make our home with them. (John 14:23).

> **If you keep my commands, you will remain in my love**, just as I have kept my Father's commands and remain in his love. (John 15:10)

This is true love, and it depends on a personal decision. It is your own decision, fully and entirely. That is why, when the Lord Jesus Christ commands you to love God with all your heart, soul, mind, and strength. In fact, He is telling you that with the deepest conviction in your heart, the strongest determination of your soul, the greatest power of your mind, and drive of your strength, to submit yourself to God, obeying him, and keeping His Word.

The love that God expects from us means serving, honoring, and above all, obeying Him. These things should demonstrate that we are capable of being true, loyal servants of God, which in fact, is our eternal mission before Him as our Lord.

When people are obedient to God, their position pleases the Lord in three of His great roles:

1. In His role as Lord, **God converts people into His servants** if they obey Him.
2. In His role as God, **He converts people into His very essence or nature**. They become part of God if they obey Him.
3. In His role as Father, **God converts people into His own sons and daughters** if they obey Him.

Clearly, obedience is the key to everything regarding God. He takes great pleasure when children obey their earthly parents. Therefore, He covers them with great blessings, because precisely, obedience is what God desires and expects from His own children. It is clear, then, that the love of God, expressed as obedience to God, is a powerful secret weapon at the disposal of every believer. Indeed, obedience to God is the only path to eternal life.

It is amazing to think that obtaining this secret weapon depends entirely and exclusively on just one thing—every individual's personal decision to obey God. Again, all you have to do is exercise your free will to accept the Lord as your God, and you will have access to that secret weapon—obedience—if you want it. Clearly, it is your own decision.

8.7. However, People Do Create Their Own Gods

After the fall of Adam and Eve, when God, through His Holy Spirit, had withdrawn himself from the human heart, the infinite infrastructure that He left in the human heart turned into a deep emptiness. Therefore, as long as the Spirit of God is not joined or coupled to the coupling station in the infinite infrastructure of the human's heart, the emptiness remains in place.

In the quest to fill the emptiness and with their hearts contaminated, hardened, and distant from God, people generally try to create or invent their own gods, hoping to fill the gaping vacuum. The trap that they most often succumb to is that their gods tend to align with the paradigms of their own natural human perceptions. Their perceptions are consistent with what they detect through their five senses.

Throughout history, people have created gods of many kinds. Some gods were celestial bodies, such as the Sun, Moon, and stars. Others were gods made of flesh and blood or some mythological hero created in their own imaginations. Likewise, others were animal figures fashioned by human hands in metal, stone, or wood. These were usually a reflection of the human desire to have gods that were visible and that could be perceived through their natural senses.

Curiously enough, after people made and create their own gods, then they ascribed supernatural powers that were beyond their own. Such gods, created by human hands, were unable to hear, see, feel, or understand.

As people block their spiritual perceptions and enthrone their natural senses, they come to believe and trust only in the things that they can see or touch; that is, what exist in their physical or natural reality, which is the only reality that they can detect with their natural senses. The resulting paradox is that people generally take part of God's creation to fashion their own gods as they overlook and ignore the creator of all things, the one and only God. Of course, the true God is invisible, and therefore, He can only be perceived by spiritual senses. Natural humans tend to have their spiritual senses blocked or atrophied, and as a result, they often have difficulty perceiving the true God. They tend to fall into this trap, to their own misfortune and God's great sorrow.

Chapter 9

THE BODY OF CHRIST

We have already seen that the body of Christ, which is also the bride of the Lamb and the church of Christ, is the union or merging of the redeemed, transformed, and revived souls of all the saved. We could say that God is a kind of super hologram and that the body of Christ is a super-soul that comprises the dwelling place of God. We will soon see that it is likewise, the great holy city of God, the New Jerusalem.

In the New Jerusalem, the relationship of co-inherency or cohabitation will take shape between God and His people, between God and His family, which will be dwelling within God, while God will be dwelling within His family, which will become His new dwelling place. Therefore, the body of Christ is simultaneously the bride of the Lamb, the church of Christ, the family of God, the city of God, God´s dwelling place and the New Jerusalem.

9.1. The New Jerusalem

There has been much discussion about what the New Jerusalem or the city of God is or represents. Some have even speculated that it is as a great physical mansion where all the redeemed of God will live. Such a description, however, is based on human paradigms.

Indeed, it is a dwelling, but it is entirely spiritual. The New Jerusalem is unlike a physical place to house God's redeemed people. When we, mere humans, tussle with the idea of divine, heavenly, and spiritual beings, we must set aside our natural senses, which will always lead us into error. The Word of God offers a few definitions of the New Jerusalem.

9.1.1. The New Jerusalem Is the Bride of the Lamb

Revelation 21:2 and 21:9–10 describe it as follows:

> I [John] saw the Holy City, the new Jerusalem, coming down out of heaven from God, prepared as **a bride beautifully dressed for her husband**. (Revelation 21:2).
>
> One of the seven angels who had the seven bowls full of the seven last plagues came and said to me, "Come, I will show you the bride, **the wife of the Lamb**." And he carried me away in the Spirit to a mountain great and high, and showed me the Holy City, Jerusalem, coming down out of heaven from God. (Revelation 21.9-10)-

The New Jerusalem is the bride that the Lord has long awaited. He is eager to hold the wedding feast and fulfill His eternal purpose of building himself a family so that He has descendants. As we have seen, this is the very purpose of all creation. **Therefore, the bride of the Lamb is called Jerusalem and she is the mother of all believers or of all God's children**. Galatians 4:26 says,

> "But the Jerusalem that is above is free, and **she is our mother**" (Galatians 4:26).

Because the Lord is the King of kings and Lord of lords, the New Jerusalem (the bride of the Lamb) will be also the queen of the kingdom of God, as the wife of any king would be. As we also saw, though, the bride of the Lamb is also the church of Christ, which is constituted by the redeemed, transformed, revived and united souls of all believers. At the same time, it is the mother of all believers or of God's children.

9.1.2. The New Jerusalem Is Also a City that Resembles Jasper

The Word of God also states that it resembles a precious stone known as jasper. Revelation 4:2–3 states,

> "At once I was in the Spirit, and there before me was a throne in heaven with someone

> sitting on it. **And the one who sat there had the appearance of jasper** and ruby. A rainbow that shone like an emerald encircled the throne." (Revelation 4:2-3).

John also describes the following in Revelation 21:10–11:

> And he carried me away in the Spirit to a mountain great and high, and showed me the Holy City, Jerusalem, coming down out of heaven from God. It shone with the glory of God, **and its brilliance was like that of a very precious jewel, like a jasper**, clear as crystal. (Revelation 21:10-11).

9.1.3. The New Jerusalem Is a City of Pure Gold in the Shape of a Cube

Revelation 21:16 and 18 says,

> "The city was laid out like a square, as long as it was wide. He measured the city with the rod and found it to be 12,000 stadia [approximately 1,380 miles or 2,220 kilometers] **in length, and as wide and high as it is long**. (Revelation 21:16).
>
> The wall was made of jasper, **and the city of pure gold**, as pure as glass." (Revelation 21:18).

9.1.4. The New Jerusalem Is God's Tabernacle and the Dwelling Place for His People

Revelation 21:3 and 22 says,

> And I heard a loud voice from the throne saying, "Look! **God's dwelling place** is now among the people, and he will dwell with them. They will be his people, and God himself will be with them and be their God. (Revelation 21:3).

> I did not see a temple in the city, because **the Lord God Almighty and the Lamb are its temple**. (Revelation 21:22).

It is clear once again that the New Jerusalem is being built out of the integration or amalgamation of redeemed, transformed, and revived souls of all believers. It is simultaneously God's tabernacle and the dwelling place of the saved. This means that God and the Lamb are the dwelling place of all believers and chosen people, who are redeemed, transformed, and revived. It is very clear and simple. God will dwell in the hearts of His redeemed souls, and they will dwell in God's heart. He is their temple, and they are His tabernacle.

This mutual dwelling between God and His people is where He lives—in the hearts of His people—and at the same time they live in God's heart. This is what we call co-inherency or cohabitation.

Again, the New Jerusalem is many things at the same time, including the bride of the Lamb, a city resembling jasper, a cube-shaped city of pure gold, and God's dwelling place or tabernacle. If God and the New Jerusalem resemble jasper, the New Jerusalem also resembles God. Anything that resembles God is either God or part of God.

Remember that when God made His people, He created them in His image and after His likeness. Genesis 1:26 says,

> "**Then God said, "Let us make mankind in our image, in our likeness**, so that they may rule over the fish in the sea and the birds in the sky, over the livestock and all the wild animals, and over all the creatures that move along the ground." (Genesis 1:26).

The human race was thus made in His own image and likeness so that God could express himself through them. In the New Jerusalem, all God's people will be the expression of Him and bear His image and appearance. All God's people will be transformed so that He can fully express himself through them. The New Jerusalem will be an indissoluble part of God.

It can be concluded, then, that the city of God, His tabernacle, His family, and the New Jerusalem, which are all exactly the same thing, are being built of those who hold the image and likeness of God. They have the piece of God's hologram in their hearts. They are chosen and transformed by the Spirit of God. In eternity, therefore, God will live in a city that is, built from the souls of all His redeemed, transformed, and revived people.

Today, every believer and local church, where Christ is preached and whose members have been transformed and converted into God's children, are miniature versions of the New Jerusalem. Every believer is being transformed, into a precious, living stone for God's universal building, the New Jerusalem, where all God's people, as a whole, will bear His image and likeness.

The bride of the Lamb will be in the New Jerusalem together with God's sons and daughters. This is because of the Inverse Hologram Principle. It says that the individual souls of believers, who are cohabiting as a single spirit with the Holy Spirit, will come together to form one great soul, which is the bride of the Lamb. At the same time, each soul, in union with the Holy Spirit, will still preserve their own integrity and individuality. They will continue to be many. All of them will become sons and daughters of God—his lineage.

For all these reasons, it should be clear that it was God who created the concept of a city long before the world was created. It is a dwelling place. God conceived the city as the dwelling where He and His people could live together. Thus, God created the New Jerusalem to serve as His dwelling place inside His people and as His people's dwelling place inside Him, in perfect co-inherency or cohabitation.

In short, the New Jerusalem is:

1. A city made up of the totality of redeemed, transformed, and revived souls of believers from all times and in perfect co-inherency or cohabitation with God.
2. The complete set of God's people in resurrection, which is an absolute or eternal state of life.
3. God's tabernacle and His people's dwelling place.
4. God's masterpiece. It is God himself with His family (wife and children). It is the bride of the Lamb, the wife of the King of kings, and therefore, it is also, the queen of God's kingdom.

In the New Jerusalem, God performed the miracle of miracles: the co-inherency or cohabitation of dwelling in the heart of His family and His family dwelling in His heart.

9.1.5. What about God's Heart?

Finally, it is important to note that God, in essence, only lives in hearts. Recall what we know about the period during the alpha God when God was alone in three persons, and He lived in His own heart.

We have also seen that when God created Adam and Eve, He lived in their hearts by means of His Holy Spirit, based on the Hologram Principle. It is clear also, that after Jesus Christ made the ultimate sacrifice to redeem humankind, people could receive Him as Lord and Savior. At that very instant; God immediately returned through His Holy Spirit to dwell in their human hearts.

Thus, the New Jerusalem is the place of co-inherency or cohabitation between God and His people. It is simultaneously the dwelling place of believers inside God and God's tabernacle inside His people, and the encounter of the redeemed, transformed, revived souls of all believers. Therefore, because God dwells in hearts and only in hearts. This leads us directly to the most significant and ultimate definition of what is the New Jerusalem:

The New Jerusalem is the very heart of God.

This, in turn, leads to a very important revelation.

When God said that David was a man after his own heart, what the Lord was really declaring was that the essence of David's heart is similar to the essence of the very heart of God.

That statement is unique and very relevant because, in those days, the hearts of men were very corrupt. They were mired in sin and very far from God. Furthermore, it was long before the shed of the redeeming blood of Jesus Christ. The above put in true dimension the statue of King David in the eyes of God. This explains also, why the Lord honored him by making Jesus the son of David and, consequently, of his lineage.

9.1.6. The New Jerusalem and the Earthly Jerusalem

We know that the earthly Jerusalem is the natural, physical, and visible Jerusalem, a place of slavery. It represents God's covenant with the children of slavery and sin. The New Jerusalem is the spiritual, the free, the heavenly Jerusalem on high that is the mother of all believers. It represents the true covenant of God's promise to His people through Abraham, His servant. You can see this in Galatians 4:22–26.

> For it is written that Abraham had two sons, one by the slave woman and the other by the free woman. His son by the slave woman was born according to the flesh, but his son by the free woman was born as the result of a divine promise. These things are being taken figuratively: The women represent two covenants. One covenant is

from Mount Sinai **and bears children who are to be slaves**: This is Hagar. Now Hagar stands for Mount Sinai in Arabia and **corresponds to the present city of Jerusalem, because she is in slavery with her children. But the Jerusalem that is above is free, and she is our mother**. (Galatians 4:22-26).

9.2. God's Pantheism

One of the philosophical and religious doctrines that tries to explain the existence of God in relation to the creation is pantheism. **It holds that god is everything and everyone, and everything is god. The universe and god are one, and the same**. The exclusively spiritual nature of God is often confused with His creation or the universe, which is temporary and in no sense forms part of God or of His kingdom.

Believers generally abhor the word *pantheism* because of the meaning it´s been given by the world. This is because they do not understand that this word or concept has been distorted to change its true spiritual meaning. In reality, it signifies an important fact about the kingdom of God, because pantheism sees its fulfillment in God and only in Him.

As we know, in the beginning, there was only God. Therefore, God was everything, and everything was God in His three persons: Father, Son, and Holy Spirit. There was no universe nor any of the things in it. Thus, if in the beginning, there was only God and everything was God, this clearly represents an initial pantheism, because in the beginning, God was everything and everyone, and everything was God. Then, God created the universe (external to himself) and everything in it, including humankind. Remember that the purpose of all creation is to form God's family—his bride and children—so that He can pour himself into His family. Once His plan and purpose are fulfilled the universe and everything in it will no longer be. Because, the universe or all creation is as a giant scaffolding that exists to serve in the construction of God's house or dwelling place, form His family, and give himself a lineage, after which, the scaffolding will be discarded.

The way things were at the beginning will return at the end. God will be everything, and everything will be God, with only one fundamental change: He will have a family. God's family will be with and in Him because it will form part of Him. Therefore, there will again be only God, and everything will be God.

This, in reality, is true pantheism. God will be everything and everyone, and everything will be God because, God will be in everything, and everything will be in God, and outside of him, nothing will exist. 1st. Corinthians 15:28 states this concept clearly:

> When he has done this, then the Son himself will be made subject to him who put everything under him, **so that God may be all in all**. (1st. Corinthians 15:28).

Pantheism is just one more example of how the enemy, by means of this world, distorts the attributes of God to make them his own and deceive people, especially believers.

9.2.1. God: Alpha and Omega

The above explained why God calls himself the Alpha and the Omega. **He is the Alpha because He is the first and the beginning. In the beginning, God was alone. There was nothing else but God, the one in three, meaning one God in His three persons**—Father, Son, and Holy Spirit.

He is the Omega because, in the end, God will be alone again but fundamentally different because His redeemed, transformed, and revived souls will be with and in Him. They will be part of God, who is God the Omega, God the three in one, three entities in a single God- the Father, His bride, and His children, all incorporated into God

himself. In a human sense, you could say that the difference between God the Alpha and God the Omega is that God the Omega will have been, enlarged with His family, the bride of the Lamb, and His children.

Thus, while the Alpha God was alone **as the God one in three, one God in three persons** (Father, Son, and Holy Spirit). The Omega God has fulfilled His mission. Therefore, He will be with His family **as the God three in one**, **three entities in one God** (the Father, His Bride, and His children).

So we move from an initial pantheism of the Alpha God to a final and everlasting pantheism of the Omega God, in which everything is God and is in God.

In the end, when the Almighty declares, it is finished, I am the Alpha and the Omega, the Beginning and the End, and then adds the First and Last, it is because once again, only God will remain, so that everything will be God. Revelation 21:6 and 22:13 says,

> He said to me: "It is done. **I am the Alpha and the Omega, the Beginning and the End**. To the thirsty I will give water without cost from the spring of the water of life." (Revelation 21:6).
>
> "I am the Alpha and the Omega, **the First and the Last**." (Revelation 22:13).

Another way of seeing the pantheism of God is by looking at the life that was only in Him since the beginning and that will only be in Him at the end. Outside of God there has never been life, there is no life, and, there never will be life, and the word *life* means eternal life. God is the only fulfillment of the concept of pantheism because outside of God there is no life.

9.2.2. Will People Ever Become God?

Once again, when God created Adam and Eve, He created them in His image and likeness, with His very essence. Because from the very beginning, His design of creation was to pour himself into Adam and Eve and to multiply himself in them so that they could be like Him and have His very essence. We have already seen that with the fall of the first man and woman, the corruption of their hearts, and their spiritual deaths, they lost the image and likeness of God—the essence of God.

God's plans and purposes never fail. So He set in motion the second phase of His plan. It would be implemented by His Own Son. Therefore, people would have another opportunity and a new path to become the essence of God, once again. Through Jesus's sacrifice and shed blood, their sins were cleansed and they were snatched from the jaws of sin and death. By means of His Holy Spirit, conditions were in place for God to return and take up residence in the human's heart, as God had at the beginning when He had first made them.

This is why receiving Jesus Christ as Lord and Savior and the Holy Spirit coming to cohabit in your heart enable God to engender you, and you are born again. This new birth is utterly different from your first biological birth. This time, you go through a spiritual birth to true life. The extraordinary thing is that you are engendered by God himself; so God becomes your Father, and you His son, and hence, you are of His lineage. Once you are God's child, like all descendants, you carry His genes—your father's essence—and acquire God's holy nature. Everyone who descends from God shares His essence. While people cannot become God on their own, they can become participants of God's divine nature, His deity, the nature of the only God.

Here, as in so many other ways, the prince of this world, the devil, seizes a divine truth and tries to make it his own by distorting it and presenting it in a way that is untrue and diabolical. It is a trap and a peril because many believers who are eager to ward off these fallacies end up shunning the great truths God has set in place.

The world speaks of a philosophical doctrine that sustains and asserts that all people are gods. This concept is utterly mistaken and far removed from the truth.

What is true, though, is that all believers will come to be God, not "a god". Instead, the very God himself who, when He invades, penetrates and saturates them with His essence, transforms them into His own fundamental nature, the divine essence of God, and thus changes them into God, the very same God who by the Hologram Principle, poured himself out into them, because there is only one God.

It is also worth remembering that when believers leave this world, their redeemed, transformed, revived souls travel to the bosom of God. They are indivisibly and indissolubly, united to the Holy Spirit for all eternity. The Lord Jesus Christ said so himself, as recorded in John 14:16.

> And I will ask the Father, **and he will give you another advocate, to help you and be with you forever**. (John 14:16).

This indissoluble bond between the Holy Spirit and the believers' souls transforms them into the image and likeness of God and therefore, into His sons and daughters. Once they are God's children, they share the same status and essence of Jesus Christ, **who is the firstborn of God, who, even being the child of man, attained heaven or the kingdom of God**. This means that, when people share the same status and essence of Jesus Christ and become coheirs of Christ, they also share the same divine quality of Jesus Christ. They share or partake in His deity.

John 17:10 records Jesus declaring that He and the Father shared all things.

> **All I have is yours, and all you have is mine**. And glory has come to me through them. (John 17:10).

Consider what the apostle Paul says in Romans 8:17.

> Now if we are children, then we are heirs—heirs of God and **co-heirs with Christ**, if indeed we share in his sufferings in order that we may also share in his glory. (Romans 8:17).

Clearly then, believers are heirs of God and coheirs with Christ. Therefore, believers' (his children's) whole selves (everything they are) belong to the Father, and the Father's whole self belongs to believers. Of course, this whole self includes God's holiness and divinity.

There is more. Remember the Lord's words in John 17:21–23, where He says,

> … **that all of them may be one, Father, just as you are in me and I am in you. May they also be in us** so that the world may believe that you have sent me. **I have given them the glory that you gave me, that they may be one as we are one—I in them and you in me—so that they**

> **may be brought to complete unity**. Then the world will know that you sent me and have loved them even as you have loved me. (John 17:21-23).

Remember that as the Son of God, Jesus Christ is God because God is full with Him and present in Him at all times. The Father and the Holy Spirit are also God because God is fully in each one of them. Because believers are coheirs with Christ and under the Hologram Principle, the Holy Spirit, who is also the fullness of God, dwells with every believer. This means that they share the same status and essence of Jesus Christ, which is the very essence of God and His deity. These believers, who have been redeemed, transformed, and revived by the same Holy Spirit who cohabits with them in their hearts and specifically in their souls, are indeed God, just as Jesus Christ is God. We already know that they are not God by themselves or a god that is different from God. They are the very same God who fully poured himself into His believers—all those who are redeemed by the blood of Jesus Christ and transformed and revived by the Holy Spirit.

This is undeniable when we recall that the Holy Spirit enters a human heart, the person's soul bonds to the Spirit of God, and the person becomes one Spirit with God. This is clear in 1st. Corinthians 6:17.

> But whoever is united with the Lord **is one with him in spirit**. (1[st.] Corinthians 6:17).

It is also worth remembering that the Father, Son, and Holy Spirit are one, and the same. 1[st.] John 5:7 explains it like this:

> For there are three that testify in heaven: the Father, the Word and the Holy Spirit, **and these three are one**. (1[st.] John 5:7).

Finally, comes the critical question: **Will people ever become God**? This is the conclusion and synthesis,

As in the case of the Hologram Principle, the Alpha God, who is one God in three, poured himself into His three persons—Father, Son, and Holy Spirit- and the three are God. Moreover, according to the Hologram Principle, the Omega God, who is the one God in many, pours himself into His sons and daughters. Therefore, each, and every one of them is God.

This means God is fulfilling His will and purpose to create His family so He can pour and multiply himself in it. Therefore, He's multiplying His divinity through His children and expressing His character as God in every one of them.

With this trait, believers will sit down with Jesus and rule with Him, because, they will be crowned as royalty and priests. Revelation 1:6 reaffirms it as follows.

> … **and has made us to be a kingdom and priests** to serve his God and Father—to him be glory and power for ever and ever! Amen. (Revelation 1:6).

In Matthew 25:33–34, Jesus uses a simile to describe the nature of God's children, who will inherit God's kingdom. It says,

> "He will put the sheep on his right and the goats on his left. Then the King will say to those on his right, 'Come, you who are blessed by my Father; **take your inheritance, the kingdom prepared for you since the creation of the world**." (Matthew 25:33-34).

Later, we will see that God himself is the kingdom of God, which will be inherited by believers. The Lord uses this simile in Matthew 25:33–34 to say that believers will inherit the very status of God. Simply put, the believers' inheritance is God himself, His essence, His divinity.

We still need to understand that when Jesus Christ was in this world still being God himself, He experienced hunger and thirst, grew tired, felt pain, was tempted, and more. In the same way and because we share the very essence of God, we will suffer all these things as long as we remain in this world. Mark 11:11–12 and John 4:6–7, 11:35 confirm some of these ideas.

> Jesus entered Jerusalem and went into the temple courts. He looked around at everything, but since it was already late, he went out to Bethany with the Twelve. The next day as they were leaving Bethany, **Jesus was hungry**. (Mark 11:11–12).

> Jacob's well was there, and Jesus, **tired** as he was from the journey, sat down by the well. It was about noon. When a Samaritan woman came to draw water, Jesus said to her, "**Will you give me a drink**?" (John 4:6–7).

> **Jesus wept**. (John 11:35).

In the same way, as long as they are in this world, believers will experience the same human feelings over and over again. They will even continue to have certain weaknesses, which often lead them to sin. The essential difference is that Jesus as human never sinned and always overcame temptation. Believers, by contrast, continue to sin from time to time. **However, they can repent, and when they do, their sins will be immediately cleansed**

by the blood of Jesus Christ, their older brother, who will care for and keep them holy before God.

The weaknesses that believers still have today, being the humans that they are, will be wiped away once they depart to God's kingdom. While they remain in this world, they cannot enjoy the fullness of God. They will enjoy a foretaste of the true godly condition that they will have in eternity. Ephesians 1:13–14 says,

> And you also were included in Christ when you heard the message of truth, the gospel of your salvation. When you believed, you were marked in him with a seal, the promised Holy Spirit, **who is a deposit guaranteeing our inheritance until the redemption of those who are God's possession**—to the praise of his glory. (Ephesians 1:13-14).

Thus, as long as believers are in this world in their mortal bodies, and have not received their new bodies transformed and revived by the Holy Spirit of God, they will still have a foretaste, an advance on the true condition that awaits them, once their souls leave this world in indissoluble union with the Holy Spirit, who will reunite with God taking the believers with Him, through the Inverse Hologram Principle.

Finally, even though Almighty God dwells with all believers through His Holy Spirit, specifically in their hearts, all too often they talk to God as if He were in some faraway place, a distant Heaven. They appear to have difficulty accepting that the only eternal God is so close by that He lives inside them. **Every believer needs to understand clearly that Heaven, the kingdom of God, is in the very same place where God is**. Because God dwells in the human heart, the kingdom of God is in the heart of every believer. Wonderful!

9.2.3. What about the Bride of the Lamb?

The bride of the Lamb is the composite of the redeemed, transformed, and revived souls of all believers, whose souls, by the Inverse Hologram Principle, combine to form a single great soul, a sort of super soul. Because she is also, united to the Holy Spirit, she shares the essence of God. God poured himself fully into her when He entered into each believer's soul, which comprises her. The bride of the Lamb, the church, will also become God, because He is pouring himself fully into her through His children. Again, it is important to emphasize that this is not some other god but the same only God. Recall, too, that the bride of the Lamb will be of one spirit with God, even as the human bride is of a single flesh with her bridegroom.

Almighty God, then, will have poured himself and expressed himself, so He will be present in all His fullness with His wife, the bride of the Lamb, and in every one of His children. Therefore, under the Hologram Principle, through His family, God is multiplying himself, as many times as there are stars in the sky or grains of sand on the ocean shores, through Abraham's descendants, and this is by faith. Later we will go into more depth on the subject of Abraham's descendants.

It is important to clarify that this multiplication of God does not mean that God will be growing because God does not grow or multiply into several gods. Instead, this is an operation of God's mathematics, in which His multiplication always equals one—one God, the same God.

This leads to two key corollaries or conclusions.

1. When people surrender their essence, their soul, to Jesus Christ, the Lord gives His own essence in exchange and equips them with His divine essence and godliness.
2. While the Alpha God is one in three, one God in three persons - Father, Son, and Holy Spirit - The Omega God is one God in many. He is the Father God poured into a bride and countless sons and daughters. They are as many as infinite.

Remember that God promised Abraham that his descendants would be like the stars in the sky and the countless grains of sand on the seashores. This was a way of saying that his offspring would be infinite in number.

The conclusion is that the Omega God is a God of infinite descent, because under the Hologram Principle, He will have poured and multiplied himself infinitely in His children while continuing to be the one and only God.

9.3. More about Jesus Christ

The Son of God, who is also God, came into the world as a man, opened a new path to the Father for us, and became the first fruits of God's people. He would be the first of all the children of man, who, being human, would eventually have and be the fullness of God. It is very simple:

> Jesus Christ, being the Son of God, became the Son of Man so that He might become the way for the children of men to become sons and daughter of God.

Jesus Christ came into the world to restore the human state, rescue us, transform us, and open a new way to God, a new way to life, a new way for us to be adopted as children of God. With the fall of Adam and Eve, humankind closed off the direct path that led to life. Thus, the only path that remained led to death.

When Jesus declared that He came to bring the kingdom of God into the world, in reality, what He brought the world was God himself. Before He left, He promised His followers that He would send God by means of the Holy Spirit, the piece of God's hologram to live with them in their hearts forever. This did not include the hearts of everyone in the world but only the hearts of those who recognized, confessed, and received Him as Lord and Savior.

What Jesus proclaimed tirelessly was that God himself had come to draw near to His people once again. Accordingly, the kingdom of God is not a place, territory, group of subjects, or sanctuary. The kingdom of God is God himself in all His splendor and majesty. The kingdom of God is God's government. Jesus stated this concept clearly in Matthew 12:28 and Luke 17:20–21.

> But if it is by the Spirit of God that **I drive out demons, then the kingdom of God has come upon you**. (Matthew 12:28).

> Once, on being asked by the Pharisees when the kingdom of God would come, Jesus replied, "The coming of the kingdom of God is not something

> that can be observed, nor will people say, 'Here it is,' or 'There it is,' **because the kingdom of God is in your midst**." (Luke 17:20–21).

We see that Jesus is at once God and human. He told them that the kingdom of God was with Him, in Him, and in their midst. He said that He himself was the kingdom of God in their midst. This was because Jesus had brought the kingdom of God to all humankind.

Thus, following the death and resurrection of Jesus Christ, now when people accept and receive the Lord into their hearts, under the Hologram Principle, the Lord moves His Kingdom with Him to dwell with that person in his or her heart to re-establish himself on His throne.

Consequently, the infinite infrastructure, which was created in the human's heart, is kindled, fanned into flame, and receives God where His empty throne once stood. Isn't it extraordinary, that the Eternal One returns to occupy His established throne, now kindled, lit up and revived in the heart of every believer? Amazing!

God's other purpose in sending His Son was so that Jesus Christ would become a visible model of God for His people to follow, emulate, and imitate. It was a visible path to follow to reach the invisible, everlasting kingdom of God.

9.4. Jesus: The Spiritual Leader versus the Political-Military Leader

Jesus did not enjoy the broad, widespread acceptance that many assumed the arrival of the Son of God would trigger, mostly among the Israelites, who represented the people of God at the time. They had been under the yoke and harsh oppression of many different nations and empires, which were at different stages of their histories, including the Egyptian Empire, the Babylonians, the Persian Achaemenid Empire, the Assyrians, and at the time of Jesus, the Roman Empire. In all these stages, they always expected the hand of God to deliver them. Now once again, they awaited a leader who would free them from Roman oppression. In reality, Jesus did not come to complete the task that their history had taught them to expect, following the same pattern that had repeated itself every time they came under the oppression of other nations.

Remember the many occasions in the book of Judges when, after constant acts of disobedience to God, the Israelites would cry out to Jehovah (YHWH), who would send them a deliverer, in this case, a judge (leader), who would free them from the hand of their oppressor. Two examples from Judges 3:7–15 serve as an illustration:

> **The Israelites did evil in the eyes of the Lord; they forgot the Lord their God and served the**

> **Baals and the Asherahs**. The anger of the Lord burned against Israel so that he sold them into the hands of Cushan-Rishathaim king of Aram Naharaim, **to whom the Israelites were subject for eight years. But when they cried out to the Lord, he raised up for them a deliverer, Othniel** son of Kenaz, Caleb's younger brother, who saved them. The Spirit of the Lord came on him, so that he became Israel's judge and went to war. The Lord gave Cushan-Rishathaim king of Aram into the hands of Othniel, who overpowered him. So the land had peace for forty years, until Othniel son of Kenaz died. **Again the Israelites did evil in the eyes of the Lord**, and because they did this evil the Lord gave Eglon king of Moab power over Israel. Getting the Ammonites and Amalekites to join him, Eglon came and attacked Israel, and they took possession of the City of Palms. The Israelites were subject to Eglon king of Moab for eighteen years. **Again the Israelites cried out to the Lord, and he gave them a deliverer—Ehud**, a left-handed man, the son of Gera the Benjamite. The Israelites sent him with tribute to Eglon king of Moab. (Judges 3:7-15).

Therefore, with their past filled with political-military deliverers, naturally, they expected their God Jehovah to send another deliverer who would save them once again in the same traditional fashion. This time their release would be from the Roman Empire, and the expected deliverer would free them from oppression and occupation over their land. Once again, they awaited a strongman, a political-military leader who, in the natural, would tear off the heavy yoke of oppression under which the Romans had subjected them. God would do the same thing that He had done when He had sent Moses to rescue them from the yoke of the Egyptians.

They did not understand that this time, the true purpose of God's promise to send a deliverer was to save their souls. This is significant because Christ came to save their souls. He would save them spiritually from eternal death and give them eternal life. The difference between the expectations of the people of Israel and God's purposes to send His Son as their Lord and Savior had consequences so profound that they remain today.

9.4.1. A Death That Brings Life

The death of Jesus Christ brought life because when He bore the sins of all people on the cross, they died to sin with Him. His resurrection made it possible for them to be born to a new life. Any person who receives Jesus Christ as Lord and Savior join Him in His death. That person dies to sin, and he or she is born to eternal life through resurrection.

Once people accept Jesus Christ as Lord and Savior, His powerful blood immediately becomes effective and cleanses them from all their sins, whether past, present, or future, and redeems them, snatching them from the jaws of death. This is the true miracle of Jesus Christ's blood. It couldn't been achieved through the blood of countless animals in sacrifice.

Even so, it is important to understand that the old nature or old self does not die immediately. It lives on, although with less intensity inside the new spiritual self. This old self lives protected by the flesh. It can't flourish, though, because it has been defeated. It lost its power when it was crucified with Jesus Christ.

As we already saw, during the period that spans from the fall of Adam and Eve to the death and resurrection of Jesus Christ, the Spirit of God could not dwell in human hearts. During those years, God did not dwell with any human at all. He was barred by the impurity of their hearts and their sinful natures.

9.5. From Natural Beings to Spiritual Beings

Remember that after the fall of Adam and Eve, all humans were born as natural beings. Consequently, they live on the earth with their natural sense. All persons, by default, are born in sin and into death without spiritual life, as sin is the spiritual death of humans. They are born separate from God. Only when they confess Jesus Christ as their Lord and Savior and receive Him into their hearts, will people gain life. We see this in 1st. John 5:12.

> Whoever has the Son has life; **whoever does not have the Son of God does not have life**. (1st. John 5:12).

However, as we already saw, the first death takes place at the first birth. It is a temporary death. God yearns and desires for people to depart from this state of temporary death in which they exist and move into a state of eternal life, of pure life. Even though the Lord desires this and fervently longs for it, God does not force, coerce, or oblige anyone. He lets them exercise their free wills and decide for themselves. They can choose to continue in the state of death in which they exist, or instead, to overcome death by being born again through Jesus Christ, who is the path that God places before all people.

Not until they receive Jesus Christ into their hearts are they born again into life. When they acquire spiritual life, they are transformed from natural creatures into spiritual beings, from death into life.

The fact that we are born spiritually dead is the very reason that Jesus came to give us true life. This is what Jesus Christ said in John 10:10.

> The thief comes only to steal and kill and destroy; **I have come that they may have life**, and have it to the full. (John 10:10).

After the fall of Adam and Eve, the only way for us to qualify to be children of God and become part of His family, the body of Christ, is to be born twice. The first birth is natural because we are born spiritually dead. The second birth is spiritual because, we are engendered by God himself through His Holy Spirit, who revives and lifts us out of our dead state into a state of true life.

On our second birth, once we are pulled out of the claws of death, and taken into the light of life, death can no longer reach us because with this second birth, we have overcome death. Of course, it was Jesus Christ, who actually overcame death for us when He vanquished it and rose again on the third day. We had no access to the second birth before the resurrection of Jesus Christ because death had not been defeated. It was the reason why, God had to protect all the righteous ones who had fallen asleep during the period that spanned, from the fall of Adam and Eve to the death and resurrection of Christ. We have already seen that God held them in a special place (Paradise) to await their second birth, which Christ would bring. Incidentally, He is the firstborn from among the dead because He was the first one who conquered death and went to the Father. This is clear in Acts 26:23.

> That the Messiah would suffer and, **as the first to rise from the dead**, would bring the message of light to his own people and to the Gentiles. (Acts 26:23).

Because Jesus was God's firstborn, by extension, He is the older brother of all believers. We are His younger brothers and sisters. Like all good older brothers, He defends, supports, and helps His younger siblings.

Something else happens when people are born again. They acquire a new home address because they shift their place of residence from the kingdom of darkness to the kingdom of God. Their new residence becomes God himself, the Omega God. The apostle Paul explains this in Colossians 1:13 and 3:3.

> For he has **rescued us from the dominion of darkness and brought us into the kingdom of the Son he loves**… (Colossians 1:13).

> For you died, and **your life is now hidden with Christ in God**. (Colossians 3:3).

When believers move into the kingdom of God, they acquire great power. Even so, many continue to behave as if they were still defeated. They fail to understand that when they were born again, they became overcomers who received the power of God. This power is far greater than any other power outside them. 1stJohn 4:4 explains it like this:

> You, dear children, are from God and have overcome them, **because the one who is in you is greater than the one who is in the world**. (1stJohn 4:4).

9.6. Death

What is death? Why has there been so much speculation and confusion about it? First, we need to distinguish between two types of death and their place in time: temporary death and eternal or final death.

9.6.1. Temporary Death

Temporary death is the provisional or temporary separation between the Spirit of God and the human soul. All people are born in this state of temporary death.

9.6.2. Eternal or Final Death

Eternal death is the perpetual, permanent, or final separation between the Spirit of God and the human soul. All people remain in this state when they leave this world without having confessed, accepted, and received Jesus Christ as Lord and Savior.

Spiritual death or death of the soul is often confused with the misnamed physical or bodily death, although they are different. Technically, there is no physical death, in view of the fact that the true concept of death involves the separation of God's Spirit from another spiritual essence, specifically, the human soul. The Spirit of God cannot unite with any physical body, so there can be no expectation that it might separate from it. Thus, physical or material things cannot experience death because they are already dead. Because true life (God) is not in them, they are separated from God, from everlasting to everlasting, that is, for all eternity.

9.6.3. Death through Separation of the Soul

From the standpoint of the separation of the soul, there are two kinds of death.

- Death through separation of the soul from sin, and
- Death through separation of the soul from the Spirit of God

Death through separation of the soul from sin occurs when a person dies to sin, and he or she is separated from it. In this way, when people are separated from sin, they are join with the Holy Spirit. Therefore, this death to sin leads to life.

Death by separation from sin that leads to life is expressed in Colossians 3:3.

> For you died [separated from sin], and **your life is now hidden with Christ in God**. (Colossians 3:3).

When Jesus bore the sins of all humankind on the cross, what He actually did was extract sins from people and take them down to Sheol. He then removed himself from them and rose to life.

Thus, separation from sin, that is, death to sin, is union with God, who is life, while separation from God is union with sin, which is death. As we have already seen, death caused by the separation of the human soul from the Holy Spirit may be either temporary or eternal.

> A key conclusion is that all people are always, conjoined and separate at the same time. In other words, if they are conjoined to sin, then, they are separate from God. Therefore, if they are conjoined to God, then, they are separate from sin.

9.6.4. Physical or Bodily Death

As we have already seen, strictly speaking, there is no physical death. Nevertheless, the term is used to express the cessation of a body's biological functions. The misnamed physical or bodily death is the process by which a person's biological functions cease, and it brings about the final separation of the soul.

If the person is a believer, the revived soul, in union with the Holy Spirit, departs from the body. In the case of an unbeliever, the soul departs from the body alone and in darkness. In both cases, the body returns to the universe, more specifically, it returns to the dust of the earth, where it came from and where it belongs. This is why it is necessary to emphasize that physical death or death of the body does not necessarily mean spiritual death or death of the soul. All those who are saved in Christ and leave this world, undergo the wrongly named physical death but not spiritual death.

9.6.5. Spiritual Death or Death of the Soul

Spiritual death or death of the soul is the state in which a person's soul is separated from the Spirit of God. This separation, as we have seen, may be temporary or eternal.

True death occurs when the soul dies, which marks the final separation between the Holy Spirit and the human soul. This is why so-called physical death can occur without spiritual death. The typical case is a believer who takes leave of this world. Spiritual death can also occur without so-called physical death. In this case, it means all people from the time they are born until they accept Jesus Christ as Lord and Savior departing from their state of spiritual death and entering into a state of true spiritual life.

Indeed, when believers leave this world, their so-called physical death takes place as their bodily functions cease. Spiritual death does not occur, and their soul is more alive than ever. So, a definition of death would be the following:

> Death is every **temporary or eternal separation** of the Holy Spirit of God from the human soul.

Anything that is separate from God is dead, and therefore, when people are born in sin, they are born separate from God and dead. This first death, which people experience at birth, however, is merely a temporary death and not a final one. If people leave the world without ever received the Lord Jesus Christ as Lord and Savior, the temporary death that was with them from birth becomes final death because of the lasting, permanent separation between the Holy Spirit and their souls.

Once again, recall that before the fall of Adam and Eve, death did not exist. Instead, they were united with God, and He was united with them in cohabitation through the Holy Spirit. It was not until their fall in disobedience that death was born. Something began to happen inside them that separated them from God and blocked Him from remaining united with His people. That something is called sin.

Death grew and multiplied because it took control of Adam and Eve, and through them, of the entire human race. People moved from light into darkness, from a state of life with Adam and Eve to a state of death that began with their fall and continued to sweep away the whole human race until today. It was so strong that before Christ, death was invincible. No human being had defeated death. It was quite the opposite. Death defeated all people. Jesus was the first person to defeat death finally. As the victor over death, Jesus gave all of us the chance for a comeback and the option of a second birth, which would defeat death for good.

Yes, Jesus gave us the possibility of defeating death because death had defeated all of us the first time that we had clashed with it, at our first birth. With the second birth, Jesus rescues and protects people from death, and it loses all power over us. He gave us the possibility to make a full U-turn, to step out of darkness into light, that is, from death to life, to be reunited with God.

Jesus was the first one to overcome death and reach the Light, reach God. He was then succeeded by all those who were in Paradise and then by all believers, who, having accepted Jesus as Lord and Savior, have since departed from this world.

This is why it has been said so often that if people are twice born, they will have to go through only one death, which occurs at birth. Those who have only one birth, though, will undergo two deaths—the first time at birth (temporary death) and the second time when they leave this world (final death).

This statement is correct and not subject to doubt. Most believers are familiar with it. What is new is that the first death occurs at the time of birth, because all people, under the original Adamic sin, are born separate from God. Lacking the piece of God's hologram in their hearts, they are born spiritually dead.

Understand, then, that people are born dead and that this first death occurs to all people at birth. The first death that people experience at birth is a temporary death. This clearly explains why Jesus is the first to have defeated death and accomplished such a crushing victory over it.

9.6.6. Jesus's Two Victories over Death

Jesus was the first to overcome death because He was the only person to defeat death twice. He achieved two victories and no losses (2 to 0). He is the only one whom death could not defeat in either of its two clashes with Him.

The first clash was at His birth. There, Jesus defeated death. Being born as the Son of God, He already had the

Holy Spirit living in His heart. This means that He was born with His piece of God's hologram. He was born in a condition similar to that of Adam and Eve when they were created, and before they fall into sinned. Therefore, He was not born spiritually dead, as the rest of us are when we are born in sin. Death had its first setback at the hands of Jesus Christ, who defeated it when He was born.

His second clash with death took place when Jesus departed this world and defeated death once again, this time permanently. He defeated death for the second time, rising again on the third day. This is the Lord's best-known mortal blow against death. Both victories are equally important and significant for the future of the human race.

Both victories together made Jesus the first person to overcome death—the first time, when He was born and when He entered the world and the second time, when He departed from the world. Death could not stop Him at His entrance or departure, and this made Him the first person never to know death at all. Another way to declare Jesus Christ´s crushing victory over death is to proclaim that Jesus is the only person who never knew sin.

The devil knew that Jesus had defeated death in His first clash with it, and knowing this, he strategically prepared his final blow so that death would beat Him on the cross. Jesus overcame death again, though, in a second and final victory.

The following fundamental fact took place at Jesus's second victory over death—the miracle that occurred with His sacrifice on the cross. There He took upon himself all the sins of the world, so much so, that the Father temporarily turned away from Him. In Matthew 27:46, the following took place when Jesus was speaking in His fully human state:

> About three in the afternoon Jesus cried out in a loud voice, "**Eli, Eli, lema sabachthani?**" (which means "My God, my God, why have you forsaken me?"). (Matthew 27:46).

Significantly, Jesus expired as a man and rose again as a man, thus dealing the final, permanent blow to death.

It should be understood that when the Bible speaks of the death of Jesus Christ and says that He died for the sins of all people and that the Father sent Him to be sacrificed for human sin, it is not talking about the death of His human soul, which is a spiritual death. Instead, it means that Jesus Christ came to die to human sin and to take upon himself the sins of all people. This is the death in reference when it says that Jesus died on the cross.

In saying that Christ died to sin, therefore, it means that He took the sins of all humankind onto himself, and with His sacrifice, He cleansed us with His own blood. Remember that Jesus was the only person born into the world without knowing death at the time of His birth, because He was born with the Holy Spirit in His heart. With His sacrifice, He bore sins that were not His own but of all people. This is the process in which, Jesus bore human sin, that, the Bible describes, saying that He died for the sins of people.

Among other things, the Lord came into this world to become the death of death. In Hosea 13:14, the prophet had already announced this.

> I will deliver this people from the power of the grave; I will redeem them from death. **Where, O death, are your plagues**? Where, O grave, is your destruction? I will have no compassion. (Hosea 13:14).

When the Lord cleansed all people from all their sins. Therefore, from death, all they had to do was accept Jesus Christ as their Lord and Savior so that they could die to their own sins, and rise to life with Jesus Christ, who opened a way, by His blood, for people to be cleansed of all their sins—past, present, and future—and die to sin with Him. Death to sin can be understood as, separation from sin.

Likewise, it is said, that people having died to life with the first Adam, rise to life with Christ, the last Adam.

It is clear, then, that all men and women are born dead. This means that in no sense can they be the temple of the Holy Spirit because the Spirit of God does not dwell in them. At birth, they are all equipped with the infinite infrastructure in their hearts so that the Holy Spirit can enter to dwell with them. This will not happen until they accept the Lord Jesus Christ as their Lord and Savior, and the Spirit of God comes to live with them and transforms them from natural beings, who are dead, into spiritual beings, who are alive. People acquire the image and likeness of God and become the temple of the Holy Spirit when they have the Spirit of God living in and with them and hold the piece of God's hologram in their hearts.

This being the case, people at birth are born dead. Their hearts are dim, in darkness and without life. However, they don't have to remain in that state; because, it is not the condition for which they were created by God. Furthermore, their first death is temporary, therefore, they only need to exercise their free wills to accept Jesus Christ as Lord and Savior, their hearts will be kindled, and the light of God will begin shining in it immediately. Death is merely temporary while life is eternal, as we read in 1stCorinthians 15:26.

> The last **enemy to be destroyed is death**. (1stCorinthians 15:26).

Before the final sacrifice that Jesus Christ made in our name, there were no means for us to be cleansed permanently from our sins. Temporary cleansing was achieved through animal sacrifice, which allowed God to move closer to us on a very limited footing. This cleansing was short-lived, so sacrifices needed to be offered constantly and continuously. When Jesus Christ made His sacrifice, His shed blood provided a way for full, permanent, and long-lasting cleansing of human sin.

The most astonishing thing about the miracle of Jesus Christ's blood is that it continues to cleanse believers of all their sins—past, present, and future. The effect is permanent and everlasting so that believers always appear free of sin and therefore, can stand holy before God.

9.7. The Mystery of the Sacrificial Blood

We have seen that from the time of Adam and Eve's fall until just prior to the death and resurrection of Jesus Christ, the people were required to offer endless animal sacrifices so that blood could be shed to cleanse their sins and prolong their lives. These sacrifices had a passing effect, which explains why they needed to be so frequent and endless.

Therefore, what is the mystery of sacrificial blood? By that time, people had a sinful nature. They were full of sin that not only separated them from God but also drove them farther and farther away from Him, pulling them ever closer to the final or everlasting death. So, God used the shed blood of sacrificial animals. He took the lives of animals—their lifeblood—to extend the lives of people. The idea was to exchange life for life and to appease God's wrath in the face of never-ending human sin, rebellion, and transgression. Of course, in both cases, this was a matter of natural life, that is, natural animal life in the blood exchanged for natural human life.

Thus with animal sacrifice, God exchanged one life for another. He used the life in the blood of animals to prolong human life and push back death.

The Lord says clearly in Leviticus 17:11 that life is in the blood.

> **For the life of a creature is in the blood, and I have given it to you to make atonement for yourselves on the altar**; it is the blood that makes atonement for one's life. (Leviticus 17:11).

This explains why God detests idols and false gods and why He is a jealous God, and commands His people not to make sacrifices to idols or the gods of men. This is because these idols and gods cannot see, hear, or feel. Above all, they are incapable of exchanging life in the blood of animal sacrifices for human life. Such sacrifice is a vain distortion of the God-given life that is in the blood. Such rituals are even more loathsome in the case of human sacrifice, which not even God demanded, as this was a sacrifice jealously guarded for one case only: Jesus, His own Son. Given God's infinite love for us, the masterpiece of His creation, and because this was all part of His plan to build a lineage, He made the dramatic decision to send His Own Son to be sacrificed so that He could redeem humankind once from all their sins and save them from death.

9.7.1. Why Was Jesus's Blood the Perfect Sacrifice?

We have already seen that life is in the blood and that God exchanged the life in animal blood for the life of His people, extending their days and protecting them from death. Given the short-lived, passing effect of the blood from animal sacrifice, God decided to send His Son, Jesus, to be sacrificed. He knew that Jesus, as God's son, had eternal life. Consequently, and contrary to the fate of blood from animal sacrifices, this blood would give people truly eternal life.

This meant that Jesus's sacrifice cleansed humankind from all their sins—past, present, and future—giving them eternal life. Let it not be forgotten, however, that an irrevocable condition still had to be met, before God could put this new phase of His plan into effect. This condition had been in place ever since He created Adam and Eve and decreed that people must always exercise their free wills to achieve the eternal lives that God offered through the sacrifice of His Son.

For all these reasons, the mystery of sacrificial blood allows God to replace the sinful lives of His people for the lives that are in animal blood. It appeases His wrath and draws people closer to himself. In the case of animal sacrifice, the effect of life in the blood is short-lived, passes quickly, and is all too brief. The sacrifice of Jesus, the Son of God, is different. The effect of the true life in His blood is permanent because it is eternal life.

9.8. What Is True Life?

So what is true life? Why haven't we acknowledged its overpowering importance? True life, eternal life, immortality, or everlasting light is the very essence of God, and it is found in Him alone.

There is no true life outside of God. What we tend to call life is nothing more than the condition that allows all of God's creatures to perform their biological functions and use their natural senses in the physical world or universe. True life exists only in God. In Him is the totality of true life, and there is none outside of Him. True life is the very essence of God. No creature has life until it receives the essence of God, who alone has it, can give it away, or dispense it. The most extraordinary and astonishing thing about this is that although God gives out true life, it remains in Him. True life does not depart from God, just as God cannot depart from himself. Therefore, anything that does not share the essence of God, is lack of true life; and anything that lacks true life is separate from God, and anything that is separate from God is dead. Another wonderful feature of the true life that exists only in God is that everything it penetrates or invades is converted to itself (true life), to the essence of God. Thus, God converts to true life, that is, to himself, all those to whom He conjoins himself. 1st. Corinthians 6:17 states this concept clearly.

> But whoever is united with the Lord **is one with him in spirit**. (1st. Corinthians 6:17).

This is the reason that when the Spirit of God invades the soul of believers, He transforms and converts them to His own essence, giving them the only true life—the same true life that is in God. Wherever there is true life it is, incorporated into God because there is none outside of God.

In short, when we accept Jesus Christ as Lord and Savior, the Lord cleanses us with His blood, the blood of Jesus Christ, and washes us of all sins, whether past, present, or future. Then the Spirit of God enters our hearts to dwell there and begins to cohabit with our soul. People who become believers receive true life, eternal life and immortality. The Holy Spirit and the human soul merge into an indissoluble whole, making us a single spirit with God, taking true life into our soul, and reviving it.

A believer whose soul is then a single spirit with God shares the essence of God, His deity, and the true life that exists only in God. The true life that believers receive into their souls is the same true life (the only one there is) that is contained in God because this true life is God himself. There is no true life outside of God, and there never can be, because true life cannot depart from God. It is His very essence, and outside of him, it does not exist.

This raises a question. How can this true life be in our own souls if it does not exist outside of God? The answer is that once, the human soul has been cleansed from, dies to, and is separated from sin, it revives. Upon revival, it is united and indissolubly enveloped in true life, and incorporated into God. Thereafter, the human soul, which has been converted into the essence of God and transformed into true life, is hidden into God. Here, it is worth remembering that under the Hologram Principle, the fullness of God, that is, the fullness of His true life is simultaneously present in all believers. At the same time, God continues to preserve His integrity and to be one alone, even as He is simultaneously present in the heart of each, and every one of His children.

This is why, when we accept Jesus Christ and receive the Holy Spirit into our hearts and He begins to cohabit with our souls, we shift from a state of death to a state of true life. Jesus reaffirms this concept very clearly in John 5:24.

> Very truly I tell you, whoever hears my word and believes him who sent me has eternal life and will not be judged **but has crossed over from death to life**. (John 5:24).

God placed everything in human hands. Even true life and death are in our hands. All we need to do is exercise our free wills and choose the right path, thereby defining our own destinies.

If the inescapable conclusion is that God alone has true life, we can more clearly understand the passage in Exodus 3:13–14. Moses asked God what answer he could give to the children of Israel when he went to them and told them that he had been sent by the God of their fathers, and they asked what His name is. God replied to Moses, "I AM who I AM." He added, "Say to the Israelites, 'I AM has sent me to you.'"

Many have been intrigued by that answer and the strange name of God—I AM. More than a few have wondered what this name of God means. To begin with, remember that God sees names as highly important and deeply representative because, a name reflects the character of its bearer. God's name is I AM because He alone *is*. If in fact He is, it is because only He truly lives and has true life. He is the God of true life. Outside of Him, there is no true life and nothing is. Like all God's names, I AM, represents one of His attributes, which is unique and exclusive. Therefore, what God actually told Moses to respond to the children of Israel was that he, had been sent by the one who truly lives, the one who has true life, that is, by the only one who is immortal. 1st. Timothy 6:16 and Revelation 1:4 express it as follows:

> ...**who alone is immortal** and who lives in unapproachable light, whom no one has seen or can see. To him be honor and might forever. Amen. (1st. Timothy 6:16).

> John, To the seven churches in the province of Asia: Grace and peace to you **from him who is, and who was, and who is to come**, and from the seven spirits before his throne. (Revelation 1: 4).

Jesus himself asserts this concept very clearly in John 14:6, when Thomas objects that if they don't know where He is going, they cannot possibly know the way. Jesus replies,

> "**I am** the way and the truth and **the life**. No one comes to the Father except through me." (John 14:6).

9.8.1. Is the Physical or Natural World Dead?

According to the definition of true life and the extensive discussion above, the following statement should come as no surprise. However, it will shake, to the core, all those who are immersed, in the natural world or who, without spiritual knowledge, continue to be steeped in their natural human understanding.

> Anyone who does not have God and therefore, does not have true life is dead. Thus, all material things are dead. **Even the universe, with all its splendor, majesty, and magnificence is dead**.

You can examine every micron, crack, gap, hole, and corner of the wide, immeasurable universe, and you will never find true life because there is no true life in it at all. The universe is dead. Please do not think that it once had true life but then died and lost its true life. No, it never had true life. It was created dead. The universe is a physical, visible world in the natural, but it is utterly separated from God, whose kingdom is spiritual and invisible. Remember that anything separate from God is dead.

9.9. Salvation in Jesus Christ Is Not Automatic

It was God who first chose us, because His desire was for us all to be His children and consequently, to form part of His family. However, God's choice does not become activated automatically. We must respond to God, exercising our free will, and accept said choice and offer.

Remember that God makes no exception of persons, but He loves everyone equally. Because of His great love, God deeply desires and wishes that all people would exercise their free wills and accept Jesus Christ as their Lord and Savior so that the Lord can enter their hearts to set up His dwelling place with them through His Holy Spirit, adopting them as His children and giving them everlasting life. God plays no favorites among people. Each, and every one, is very special to Him.

Human salvation is as simple as this: God yearns for your heart or more specifically, your soul. However, He leaves the decision in your own hands. He allows you to decide whether you want to be saved or you don't. If you choose salvation, you receive the Lord into your heart and thus receive the Holy Spirit, your piece of God's hologram, who hitches to your soul and merges with it. The Holy Spirit then transforms and restores your soul. When you leave this world, that same Spirit takes your soul with Him to the bosom of God. Remember that the Holy Spirit, the piece of God's hologram is, as your admission ticket, passage, or passport, which you need if you are to achieve salvation and to be united to the church of God, the bride of the Lamb.

By contrast, those who choose to turn down God's offer cannot receive the Holy Spirit. Therefore, they will have no one to transform and restore their souls and make them acceptable to God. They will not have the admission ticket or valid passport that is essential to enter into the arms of God. They will despise their salvation and be lost.

Some people believe and mistakenly insist that if Jesus Christ bore all human sins on the cross, His sacrifice cleansed everyone and freed them from their sins, and therefore, all people will achieve salvation, no matter what happens or what they do. This belief is utterly wrong and very dangerous, as it is a misinterpretation of Jesus's sacrifice.

The fact of the matter is that we were all, expelled from God's glory. So, there is no human means of achieving salvation, given the sinful state in which natural humans live. What the sacrifice of Jesus Christ actually did was to give us all, without exception, the opportunity or the choice to be completely cleansed of all our sins, whether past, present, or future. In order for this cleansing to be activated and for it really to happen, we need to explicitly accept the offer that Jesus Christ extends to us. Again, it is essential for all of us to use our free wills and accept Jesus Christ as our Lord and Savior.

9.10. God's Mercy and Grace and Jesus Christ's Death and Resurrection

Until a few years ago, many believers placed greater stress on the death of the Lord Jesus Christ than on His resurrection. They tended to exalt the value of the sacrifice that He made when He gave up His life for the salvation of all. More recently, this emphasis has shifted to His resurrection, underscoring the fact that if Jesus Christ had not risen, He would be a dead god, and believers would have no future whatsoever. The fact is that neither event outranks the other, because both are expressions of the infinite love of God for humankind. They are both equally significant and of equal rank, much like the two sides of a single coin.

The mercy and grace of Jesus Christ are fully expressed with His death and resurrection. The death of Jesus Christ was the greatest expression of God's mercy for His people because when Jesus Christ took everyone's sin upon himself, He set people free from the death that they deserved as punishment for their many sins.

At the same time, the resurrection was the greatest expression of God's grace for His people, because, He revived them and gave them eternal life, which none of us deserved, since there is nothing we can do for ourselves to gain eternal life.

In short, Jesus Christ, with His infinite mercy, died to set us free from the death that we deserved, and with His infinite grace, He rose again to give us the eternal life that we did not deserve.

It is clear, then, that neither of these two expressions of Jesus Christ's great love—his mercy nor grace—stands above the other, but they are two sides of the same coin. Both are equally significant and essential for our final destiny.

9.10.1. The Baptism of John and the Baptism in Jesus

John's water baptism was a very important and symbolic baptism because it represented death to sin. It was a baptism that invited people to repentance and to have faith in the one who was to come (Jesus Christ). Acts 19:4 explains it like this:

> Paul said, "John's baptism was **a baptism of repentance. He told the people to believe in the one coming after him**, that is, in Jesus." (Acts 19:4).

Indeed, John's baptism symbolically represented repentance, cleansing of the heart, and the faith that people would need to have in the coming Messiah. It was a symbolism or representation of the true baptism that Jesus would bring and establish among all people. This is because John's baptism did not transform the human heart or cleanse it from sin. No blood until that time had been able to wipe away past, present, and future sin, once, and for all. Bear in mind that only in the presence of this essential condition can the Holy Spirit, the piece of God's hologram, enter in and dwell in human hearts.

Both conditions apply to baptism in Christ Jesus—cleansing from sin and the subsequent entering in of the Holy Spirit to dwell in the human heart. Furthermore, baptism ceased to be symbolic in Jesus Christ and became a true process of human transformation. It became the process by which, we die to sin, and we are born to life. This baptism occurs when believers confess and accept Jesus Christ as Lord and Savior and receive Him into their hearts.

It is also a baptism in the Spirit, with whom light enters, kindles, illuminates, and revives the human heart, and casts out all darkness, including sin, thus expelling death from all hearts. Many believers assume that John's water baptism is a commandment, failing to understand that it is not a prerequisite to obtain salvation. In fact, they confuse John's water baptism, which is symbolic, with the baptism of Jesus Christ, which is a requirement for obtaining salvation. What we need to understand is that water baptism, John's baptism, is symbolic and is not essential for obtaining salvation. Nevertheless, if believers wish to combine their baptism in the Spirit with the symbolism of John's water baptism, it certainly will do them no harm. True baptism, though, the one that saves and for which we all must strive, is baptism in Jesus Christ. It does not necessarily include water, but instead, it is a process of miraculous transformation, that takes place in our hearts when we confess Jesus Christ as Lord and Savior.

A typical case of salvation without water baptism and that occurs with some frequency is when unbelievers are at death's door, and just before their final departure, they accept and confess Jesus Christ as Lord and Savior. There is no time for water baptism, but these people do receive salvation.

Finally, remember that Romans 10:9–10 outlines the requirements to be saved.

> If you declare with your mouth, "Jesus is Lord," and believe in your heart that God raised him from the dead, you will be saved. For it is with your heart that you believe and are justified, and it is with your mouth that you profess your faith and are saved. (Romans 10:9-10).

It is clear, then, that water baptism is not a condition or prerequisite for salvation. It certainly does no harm. Nevertheless, it may be useful to believers as a symbol by which they promise to submit to the change of life that the Lord is beginning to work in them, through the Holy Spirit, once He enters to dwell in their hearts.

9.11. Temptation

Temptations are tests that people must face throughout their sojourn in this world. Temptations serve to test our faith, mettle, and character. The purpose of faith, in turn, is to save our souls. This is specified in 1st. Peter 1:5 and 9.

> …who through faith are shielded by God's power **until the coming of the salvation that is ready to be revealed in the last time.** (1st. Peter 1:5).
>
> …**for you are receiving the end result of your faith, the salvation of your souls**. (1st. Peter 1:9).

Temptation is natural in the human life, and God does not let us to be tempted beyond what we can resist and overcome. The way to overcome temptation is always to safeguard our close relationship with God.

Even Jesus was tempted, but He always resisted and overcame temptation and never gave into it. Temptation is something that God allows into our lives, and it serves several purposes, which includes, building our character, solidifying our faith, and giving us the opportunity to exercise our free wills.

The devil and his demons watch, search, spy on, and observe us closely so that they can figure out what our main strengths and weaknesses are. If they know our weaknesses, they can tempt us in the very areas where we are vulnerable and more likely to fall into sin. If they know our strengths, they can interfere with God's work in us and hinder our progress in the kingdom of God. This is why we are all tempted in our areas of greatest weakness and at the same time, sifted in our areas of greatest strength. This is how the strength of our faith is tested. We all are often, challenged with powerful temptations, especially in our weakest areas. Sometimes we may fall and get back up, but regardless of the outcome, we all go through temptations.

Furthermore, the devil tends to tempt believers in all three of their essences—physical dimension, spiritual dimension, and soul. He tempted Jesus himself three times. The first time was in the desert, the second was at the top of the temple, and the third was on a high mountain.

1. He first tempted Jesus's physical essence, seizing the opportunity when Jesus was hungry after a forty-day fast.

2. He then tempted Jesus's spiritual essence by attacking His faith.
3. Finally, he tempted His soul by appealing to His ego and pride.

All three times, Jesus resisted and overcame temptation. He did so by taking refuge in the Word of God. To resist and overcome temptation, believers always need to be on the alert and clearly aware of every time that they are being tempted. Then they must lean on the Lord and His Word.

The reason that many people fall into temptation or are overcome by it, is because, their relationship with God is nearly always weak or at least not strong enough to give them the power, conviction, and strength that they need to fight temptation. While it is never a sin to come under temptation, it is a transgression to let ourselves be overcome by it. Without exception, we have all been tempted, and we will be again while we are in this world. No one has entirely been free of temptation. This is because temptation is a test that God allows in our lives to strengthen His relationship with us, build our characters, and allow us to exercise our free wills.

Never forget that everything that happens is done or allowed by God. Nothing takes place outside His sovereign will or purposes. In the specific case of temptation, God does not tempt anyone, but He does allow us to be tempted.

God's formula for you to resist and overcome temptation is to submit yourselves to Him and pray. Submission to God will give you the conviction power, ability, and strength that you need to resist temptation. James 4:7 explains it like this:

> Submit yourselves therefore to God. **Resist the devil and he will flee from you**. (James 4:7).

When you submit to God, you receive the strength and power that you need to resist and overcome everything—temptation, fear, and weaknesses. Thus when people submit to God, He unleashes His power in them through His Holy Spirit. The devil cannot withstand this power. Instead, he flees from its presence.

If believers want to avoid entering into temptation, they need to pray. This is what Jesus says in Luke 22:40 and 46.

> On reaching the place, [Jesus] said to them, "**Pray that you will not fall into temptation**." (Luke 20:40).

> "Why are you sleeping?" [Jesus] asked them. "Get up and **pray that you will not fall into temptation**." (Luke 20:46).

When the Holy Spirit enters your heart to dwell with you, God's immense power may or may not manifest in you, depending on the priority that you give the Lord in your life or the place where you hold God in your heart. All too often and even with the Holy Spirit dwelling in their hearts, some people allow their sinful nature to resurface, rise up, and grieve the Holy Spirit, who is cornered in their hearts. In other cases, the believer's agenda often conflicts with God's agenda, and almost inevitably, that agenda takes precedence over the Lord in his or her heart.

However, when believers diminish themselves and allow the Holy Spirit to grow in them and take primacy in their hearts above everything else, they finally receive the power of the Spirit, which grows and manifests itself powerfully in them. Thus, they acquire the condition that enables them to perform signs, prodigies, and miracles, as the Lord desires.

On the contrary, the power of the devil grows powerfully in people's lives. This power becomes invincible for them when they remain indifferent to and far from God. So, that same power of the devil becomes null and insignificant when they submit themselves to God. The devil has authority only over the natural person (the spiritually dead soul) because his only authority over us as believers is what we ourselves yield to him. We believers are always mindful that Jesus Christ overcame the devil and took back for us, the authority over all things in this world, which God first gave Adam and Eve when He created them.

9.11.1. God's Purpose for Stumbling Blocks and Adversities in the Lives of Christians

Stumbling blocks, obstacles and adversities are part and parcel of human life. They are intrinsic to our existence and inevitable in our journey through this world. Some obstacles and adversities are self-generated because they stem from our own decisions. Others come from the outside, and we have little control over them.

We believers often react to adversity with annoyance, anger, and frustration. We often wonder why God allows stumbling blocks, obstacles and adversities in a believer's life. The answer is very simple: True character, temperance, self-control, perseverance, compassion, and most positive human qualities develop only in the midst of stumbling blocks and adversities. Remember that gold is purified only in the presence of fire. In the same way, the fire of adversity and obstacles is God's tool for strengthening, purifying, and refining the human character.

It´s been said so many times, and it is still true today, that adversities are blessings in disguise. If this is true, we should adopt an attitude that is less negative and pessimistic, and instead, we should become positive and even hopeful every time a new adversity appears in our paths. If God allows adversity in human life for our good, the best response that we can have from now on is to accept and even welcome the benefits that adversity brings into our lives. Why not? We must learn to anticipate and even welcome the blessings that troubles and adversities will bring into our lives, although they cause us to trip, stumble, or fall.

What do we know about God's purposes when He allows these tests into our lives? What do we really know at all? As in the case of His servant, Job, it may just be that the Lord is so pleased with and proud of us that He allows us to be subjected to testing, thus demonstrating the reason why He is pleased and satisfied with us, His servants. If this is so, wouldn't it be better for us to rise to the test and overcome it as Job did? Wouldn´t it be appalling to fail the test, disappoint the Lord, grieve and sadden the Spirit?

In the end, we believers know that we cannot journey through this world without affliction. Instead, the Lord Jesus Christ himself has clearly warned that we must absolutely expect to have troubles. He never said that we might possibly just come across a few obstacles, perplexities, difficulties, or challenges in our earthly pilgrimages. No, the Lord assured us that we would definitely have troubles. These are Jesus's words in John 16:33:

> I have told you these things, so that in me you may have peace. **In this world you will have trouble**. But take heart! I have overcome the world. (John 16:33).

The Lord's warning is clear and unvarnished. The good in all this is the hope that He himself gives us when He asks us to simply trust Him and have peace because He has overcome the world. Once again, we see the Lord's character and His seal in the scriptures. He always wants to see us take the first step of faith and demonstrate our trust in God. After that, the Lord springs into action, and our victory is assured. His seal is clearly stamped with indelible ink in His Word.

Chapter 10

THE KINGDOM OF GOD, COINCIDENCE, AND THE DUAL DIMENSION OF GOD'S WORD

There are no coincidences in the kingdom of God. If people pray to the Lord and place a petition before Him in faith, and that petition is within His sovereign will, the Lord assigns it a given priority. In His time, He makes all the arrangements, preparations, and connections that are necessary to align the people, events, resources, agents, and factors that need to intervene, in the natural as in the spiritual, for that petition to receive the right response at the right time.

Indeed, because God is omniscient, He knows in advance, what we will ask Him, and He often makes the preparations and lines up the circumstances long before we even make our request. Certain preparations were already in place long before we were born, and others were there before the very founding of the world.

Remember that we are in the presence of the only God, who knows everything and can do anything. Nothing happens unless He orders it to be or allows it. As it happens, many people, especially unbelievers, see these divine acts of God and describe them as coincidences or luck. Neither luck, nor coincidence exist in God's kingdom. The Lord coordinates everything and answers His people's petitions. This is what we read in Ephesians 2:10:

> For we are God's handiwork, created in Christ Jesus to do good works, **which God prepared in advance for us to do**. (Ephesians 2:10).

Believers must bring to bear three ingredients when they have a petition for the Lord. These are the following:

1. Faith—you must ask with faith.
2. Obedience—you must be obedient to God.
3. The step of faith—you need to take the first step of faith.

If you lack faith, you will not ask with conviction or believe in the depths of your heart that you can receive a favorable reply to your petition. God wants you to believe, in the deep of your heart, that He exists. He wants you to be fully convinced that He is almighty and that He can do anything that lies within His sovereign will to answer our pleas. The Word states clearly that it is impossible to please God without faith.

As for obedience, what God most desires from you is to love Him by obeying Him, submitting to His will, and keeping

His Word. God does not make it a practice of answering petitions of disobedience. This is because disobedience is one of the worst possible ways for us to reject God.

Finally, depending on what you are asking, God generally waits for you to take the first step of faith. A step of faith is a sign that you trust in Him fully. Once you take that first step, God responds to your faith many times over and grants your requests.

The Bible gives examples, such as the story of the priests who, carrying the Ark of the Covenant, stepped out in faith to wade into the Jordan River, which was at flood stage. Before their feet even touched the water, God opened a way for them between the waters, and the priests crossed over on dry land while bearing the ark.

10.1. The Dual Dimension of God's Word

When God speaks with us and makes promises, His Word and His promises nearly always have two dimensions.

1. A temporal dimension in the physical or natural world.
2. A spiritual or eternal dimension.

This means that God's Word and promises have both time-bound and eternal effects. It is my own view, one in which I have not received revelation, that God does this to impact the believer's dual temporal and spiritual condition.

One of the problems that we have had in our relationship with God over time has been our one-dimensional understanding of God's Word. It seems that we nearly always focus exclusively on the temporal dimension, even though the eternal, spiritual dimension is so much more important. This has been happening ever since Abraham and it has not changed. This truth merits closer attention, and I would like to illustrate it with a few examples.

10.1.1. The Promised Land

God first spoke about the Promised Land to the patriarchs Abraham, Isaac, and Jacob, and later, to the children of Israel. He had plans to give the patriarchs' physical or natural descendants a physical, natural, or temporal nation here on Earth. Many years later, Joshua ushered the people of Israel into that very inheritance. In fact, the promise also had a spiritual dimension that targeted a heavenly land, a homeland, an eternal dwelling place where God's people could live with Him forever. This spiritual and eternal dimension was actually the essence or core of the original promise.

10.1.2. Abraham's Descendants

When God promised Abraham that his descendants would be like the stars in the heavens and the countless grains of sand on the seashore, He was not speaking only of a physical or carnal lineage, which would also become very numerous. God was particularly and essentially pointing to Abraham's spiritual lineage, that is, his descendants by faith. In Romans 4:11 and Galatians 3:7 and 29, this concept is clearly articulated. The Apostle Paul says the following with reference to Abraham in Romans 4:11.

> And he received circumcision as a sign, a seal of the righteousness that he had by faith while he was still uncircumcised. So then, he is **the father of all who believe but have not been circumcised**, in order that righteousness might be credited to them. (Romans 4:11).

He adds,

> Understand, then, **that those who have faith are children of Abraham. If you belong to Christ, then you are Abraham's seed**, and heirs according to the promise. (Galatians 3:7, 29)

Clearly when God spoke in His eternal vision of Abraham's lineage, He was talking about a people made up of all believers. This means Abraham's true descendants are his spiritual children. This also explains and sheds light on the reason why God ordered the people of Israel not to mix with the peoples around them. These groups were not descendants of Abraham but of slavery. They were not children by faith, and they held to and believed in other gods.

God foresaw all this and ordered the Israelites not to turn to the right or to the left from the road that He had marked out for them. Their sons should not marry the daughters of the neighboring tribes neither should their daughters be given in marriage to the men of these other nations. All this was because God did not want the faith of the Israelites to be contaminated with beliefs of pagan gods. He did not want His people Israel to abandon Him as their God and take on the pagan gods of their neighbors.

God was not talking about contamination of the body or physical contamination but rather, contamination of their faith or spiritual contamination so that they would not turn away from Him. Over the years, all too often, the commandment that God gave the Israelites has been misinterpreted. They charge the people of Israel with discriminating against other peoples by refusing to allow their children to intermarry with the children of pagans.

The Bible even gives clear evidence that God was not concerned about contamination on the physical plane but contamination of their faith, as exemplified by Rahab the prostitute and Ruth, Naomi's daughter-in-law. Both were pagans. Yet both believed and adopted the faith and the God of Abraham. They became part of his lineage and ultimately, pillars among the people of God. Even more compelling is that the Lord Jesus Christ, the firstborn son of God, descended from both of them. This is what we read about Rahab in Hebrews 11:31 and the story of Ruth in Ruth 1:15–16:

> By faith the prostitute Rahab, **because she welcomed the spies, was not killed with those who were disobedient**. (Hebrews 11:31).

> "Look," said Naomi, "your sister-in-law is going back to her people and her gods. Go back with her." But Ruth replied, "Don't urge me to leave you or to turn back from you. Where you go I will go, and where you stay I will stay. **Your people will be my people and your God my God**. (Ruth 1:15–16).

As you can see and appreciate, these two women shared a willingness to embrace the faith of Abraham, and this decision transformed them into his descendants.

Therefore, Abraham's most important lineage is not his physical or natural descendants of the flesh but rather, his spiritual lineage, that is, his descendants by faith. All believers, whether Jews or gentiles, are descended from Abraham, and they will reach the true Promised Land, which is salvation or the eternal life that was promised to Abraham's descendants by faith. Once again, this example shows the dual dimension of God's Word and His promises.

10.1.3. God's People

It is important to stress that Israel represents the people of God. Although this originally meant Abraham's physical offspring, Israel turned out to be only the first seed of God's great people, which eventually embraced all believers.

Today, however, the expression "people of Israel" no longer refers only and exclusively to the descendants of Abraham, Isaac, and Jacob by the flesh. Instead, the people of Israel now comprise the full spectrum of God's people who have descended from Abraham, Isaac, and Jacob by faith or the Spirit.

This means that the children of Israel are no longer only the traditional Israelites but all believers. Ephesians 2:12–19 says,

> At that time you were separate from Christ, **excluded from citizenship in Israel** and foreigners to the covenants of the promise, without hope and without God in the world. But now in Christ Jesus you who once were far away have been brought near by the blood of Christ. For he himself is our peace, who **has made the two groups one** and has destroyed the barrier, the dividing wall of hostility, by setting aside in his flesh the law with its commands and regulations. **His purpose was to create in**

> **himself one new humanity out of the two**, thus making peace, and in one body to reconcile both of them to God through the cross, by which he put to death their hostility. He came and preached peace to you who were far away [the gentiles] and peace to those who were near [traditional Israelites]. For through him we both have access to the Father by one Spirit. Consequently, **you are no longer foreigners and strangers, but fellow citizens with God's people and also members of his household**. (Ephesians 2:12-19).

Eventually, the two people became one through Jesus Christ and by faith. The natural-born Israelites are the people known as Israel, the descendants of Abraham, Isaac, and Jacob (Israel) by the flesh. But in reality, the Israelites, in the spiritual sense, are all God's people, made up of the whole body of believers. These are the descendants of Abraham, Isaac, and Jacob (Israel) by faith.

10.1.4. The Baptism of John the Baptist

We have already seen that John's baptism was a ceremony that beckoned people to repentance and this is why it was so important. In fact, though, it is a symbol. No one receiving this baptism achieved salvation or eternal life, because it was a natural baptism, not a spiritual act.

John's baptism was a symbol of what would be the true baptism in spirit that Christ was to introduce for the remission of sins among all people, who would be reborn and gain eternal life. Baptism is yet another illustration of the dual dimension (temporal and spiritual) of God's Word.

10.1.5. Jesus Is the Bread of Life

When Jesus declared that He was the bread of life that had descended from heaven, He said that anyone who ate of that bread would live forever. He added that the bread He was offering was His body, which He would give up for the life of the world. What did He mean? What is the other dimension of this message that was spoken by the Lord? We should examine His exact words in John 6:35, 48, and 51.

> Then Jesus declared, "**I am the bread of life**. Whoever comes to me will never go hungry, and whoever believes in me will never be thirsty." (John 6:35)
>
> "**I am the bread of life**." (John 6:48)
>
> "**I am the living bread that came down from heaven. Whoever eats this bread will live forever. This bread is my flesh, which I will give for the life of the world.**" (John 6:51)

When Jesus said this, in no sense did He mean that He was physical bread that we would literally eat. Instead, He was referring to himself as the Savior of the world and the one who gives true life to those who accept and receive Him into their hearts as Lord and Savior. He was the one who could give true life to the spiritually dead, which, until that time, was the condition of everyone since the fall of Adam and Eve.

10.1.6. The Passover

When God established the Passover for the people of Israel in Egypt, He used the blood of a lamb sprinkled on the doorframes of the Israelites' houses to save them from death. In this case, it was physical death. The Passover was also a symbol of the true Passover that would be celebrated with Jesus Christ, the Son of God, as the Lamb of God, whose blood would save humankind, not from physical death but from spiritual or eternal death. This blood would save people from eternal death, giving them eternal life in exchange.

These are only a few examples that illustrate and confirm the two-way effect—the dual dimension of the temporal and spiritual or eternal condition of God's Word and His promises.

Chapter 11

MODERN-DAY BELIEVERS AND THE EARLY CHRISTIANS' POWER AND AUTHORITY

There is no question that, the early Christians displayed great power and authority through the signs, wonders, and miracles that they wrought. It is strange to think that today's believers, in general, do not demonstrate the same level of power or authority that was displayed in the primitive church.

Keep in mind that the early Christians had a special quality that empowered them to perform great signs, wonders, and miracles—the filling of the Holy Spirit. This was how the Lord combined His Word with these signs. As if it were the most natural thing in the world, they healed the sick, cast out demons, gave sight to the blind, straightened paralyzed legs, and raised the dead.

Remember that at first, the apostles had not yet received the Holy Spirit. Even afterward, they still had not yet fully consolidated the power to perform these wonders. It was not until Pentecost, when they were filled with the Holy Spirit, that they acquired the fullness of that power.

Why don′t today′s Christians see the signs, wonders, and miracles that so often attended the early Christians? Isn’t it the same kingdom of God? Isn′t this still a kingdom of power?

Look at Mark 16:16–18 and remember that just before His departure, Jesus told the apostles,

> Whoever believes and is baptized will be saved, but whoever does not believe will be condemned. **And these signs will accompany those who believe: In my name they will drive out demons; they will speak in new tongues; they will pick up snakes with their hands; and when they drink deadly poison, it will not hurt them at all; they will place their hands on sick people, and they will get well**. (Mark 16:16-18).

As we know, believers in the early church did just what Jesus had said. They performed these signs, wonders, and miracles. Mark 16:20 continues in the same vein.

> Then the disciples went out and preached everywhere, **and the Lord worked with them and confirmed his word by the signs that accompanied it**. Amen. (Mark 16:20).

We see that wherever the Lord’s disciples went, He helped them and backed up His word with these signs.

Not only that, but we can find many other scriptures that reaffirm how these signs followed the early believers: Acts 2:43; 5:12, 14–16; 6:8; 8:6–8, 13; 9:17–18; 19:11–12; 1 Corinthians 4:20. The following passage describes what happened at Pentecost, just after the apostles received the filling of the Holy Spirit and Peter spoke to the crowd.

> Everyone was filled with awe **at the many wonders and signs performed by the apostles**. (Acts 2:43).

Acts 5:12, 14–16 describe what happened when the apostles were gathered together, and Ananias and Sapphira brought them part of the proceeds from the sale of an inheritance.

> The apostles **performed many signs and wonders among the people.** And all the believers used to meet together in Solomon's Colonnade. (Acts 5:12).

> Nevertheless, more and more men and women believed in the Lord and were added to their number. As a result, people brought the sick into the streets **and laid them on beds and mats so that at least Peter's shadow might fall on some of them as he passed by**. Crowds gathered also from the towns around Jerusalem, bringing

> their sick and those tormented by impure spirits, **and all of them were healed**. (Acts 5:12, 14-16).

The next passage, from Acts 8:6, describes the kind of person that Stephen was when the apostles appointed him and six other men of good witness, who were full of the Holy Spirit, to serve as the first deacons of the first church.

> **Now Stephen**, a man full of God's grace and power, **performed great wonders and signs among the people**. (Acts 6:8).

Later after Stephen's death, Acts 8:6–8 and 13 describe what happened when the great persecution of the church began and the believers were scattered.

> When the crowds heard **Philip** and saw the signs he performed, they all paid close attention to what he said. For with shrieks, impure spirits came out of many, **and many who were paralyzed or lame were healed**. So there was great joy in that city. (Acts 8:6-8).

> Simon himself believed and was baptized. And he followed Philip everywhere, **astonished by the great signs and miracles he saw**. (Acts 8:13).

Acts 9:17–18 narrates significant events that took place after Saul had his first encounter with Jesus on the road to Damascus.

> Then **Ananias** went to the house and entered it. Placing his hands on Saul, he said, "Brother Saul, the Lord—Jesus, who appeared to you on the road as you were coming here—**has sent me so that you may see again and be filled with the Holy Spirit." Immediately, something like scales fell from Saul's eyes, and he could see again**. He got up and was baptized. (Acts 9:17-18).

Acts 19:11–12 portrays God's power working even through the garments worn by the apostle Paul when he arrived at Ephesus.

> God did extraordinary miracles through Paul, so that even **handkerchiefs and aprons that had touched him were taken to the sick, and their illnesses were cured and the evil spirits left them**. (Acts 19:11-12).

Finally, the following passage was taken from the first letter that the apostle Paul sent to the Corinthians about the power of the kingdom of God. 1st. Corinthians 4:20 says:

> **For the kingdom of God is not a matter of talk but of power**. (1st. Corinthians 4:20).

As we can see, for the most part, the believers in the early church were filled with the Holy Spirit, and the power of God followed them in the form of signs such as miracles and wonders.

The main reason why modern Christians rarely display the power or authority seen in the early church—even though the Holy Spirit is dwelling in their hearts—is that too many of today's believers do not have the filling of the Holy Spirit. The main reason that they do not have this is because God´s Holy Spirit is usually grieved and therefore, barricaded in a back corner of believers' hearts. They find themselves obeying people more than God, even though, every believer's primary obligation is to obey God above all else. In Acts 5:29, Peter and the apostles referred to this, when they were ordered to stop teaching and preaching Jesus Christ.

> Peter and the other apostles replied: "**We must obey God rather than human beings!**" (Acts 5:29).

Over time, we have fallen into the deep pit of materialistic humanism, where human beings place their material goods at the center of their lives and keep God, His Word, and consequently, His will at bay. The tragedy is that many believers, gradually and almost inadvertently, have let themselves swept along in this materialistic-humanistic tide, which grieves the Holy Spirit and barricades Him into a remote corner of their hearts. All too often, believers end up on "the other side of the street", and without even realizing it, they find themselves on the opposite team, limiting, hindering, and even opposing God.

The fact is that over time, the materialistic-humanistic philosophy has taken power over much of the human heart. As they cling to this philosophy, many believers do not have the necessary anchorage, and they are not sufficiently rooted and grounded in the Lord. Therefore, they are, not separated nor protected against this and other alien currents. Like all natural beings, they are, dragged along in strange waters, which end up invading and polluting their hearts. Faced with this invasion of materialistic-humanism in their hearts, believers gradually find their faith growing cold. As their faith weakens, they let down their guards and become defenseless. Finally, they begin yielding to humanistic doctrines and adopt them for themselves, without realizing that they have become, distanced and separated from God.

Materialistic-humanism has transformed people into a sort of a drifting sailboat without anchor nor rudder. It has no clear path. It is swayed here and there, back and forth, depending on the intensity and direction of whatever wind is blowing at the time.

This contamination of the hearts of today's believers grieves the Holy Spirit, who finds himself barricaded or marginalized in their hearts. Under such conditions, they cannot receive the fullness of the Holy Spirit, which is a necessary condition for a believer to gain full access to the power, authority, and support of the Lord to see signs, wonders, and miracles.

Thus, if today's believers are to have power and authority and see signs, wonders, and miracles following them, the key is that they believe God, obey him, and give Him first place in their lives, above all else. This attitude will create the necessary conditions for believers to be filled with the Holy Spirit. Holy Spirit filling, in turn, will activate the power and authority within them to perform signs, wonders, and miracles, just as the early Christians did.

God gives His Holy Spirit as a gift to all who confess Jesus as Lord and Savior. The Holy Spirit promotes and renders great works through all those who obey the Lord. He even gives them unlimited power and authority.

Therefore, when you allow materialistic-humanism to pollute your heart, you lose all capacity to exercise the power that God has given to you, even as a believer for the following reasons:

1. You do not know God's Word or know it only in part. This can be corrected easily by simply reading, studying, and searching the scriptures daily.

2. You do not protect or guard your heart against wrong thoughts that are often triggered by negative emotions. They produce bad feelings and lead you to make poor decisions, which yield bad fruit.

   Proverbs 4:23 stresses the absolute need to protect your heart:

   Above all else, **guard your heart**, for everything you do flows from it. (Proverbs 4:23).

3. Believers obey other people instead of obeying God, which is your first obligation above, and beyond any other person or thing.
4. Believers do not exercise their faith. Faith is exercised by believing God and taking constant steps of faith.
5. Believers do not practice ongoing fellowship with God by creating the habit of staying in regular relationship with the Holy Spirit. It is a good habit to remain connected to the Lord at all times and not only at specific moments. You should be constantly aware that the Lord is with and in you.

In short, believers should draw near to God, submit to Him, and take refuge in Him at all times. They should live under His mighty, sheltering wings.

Once again, it is worthy to look at James 4:7–8.

> Submit yourselves therefore to God. Resist the devil and he will flee from you. Come near to God and he will come near to you. (James 4:7-8).

When you remain in God's will and obey Him under all circumstances, the following will happen:

1. The Holy Spirit will take pleasure and delight in you. As a result, He will dwell with you in your heart and make it His home. This pleasure and delight is one of the factors that generates the fullness of the Holy Spirit and causes Him to unleash His great power through believers.
2. Your face will shine with a special light. Instead of looking harsh and angry, you will take on a sweet expression because you are relaxed, amiable, and fresh—in short, your face will be angelic. You will lose all trace of the hardness, which is so common among natural persons who draw on their own strength and obey other people instead of God.

We find a description of such a face in the story of Stephen, who was filled with the Holy Spirit when, he was being judged by the council in Acts 6:15.

> All who were sitting in the Sanhedrin looked intently at Stephen, and they saw that his face was like the face of an angel. (Acts 6:15).

11.1. The Consequences That Come from a Believer's Lack of Power and Authority

God wants to give power and authority to all believers, His children. His desire is to train and equip them to do good and fight evil, which means healing the sick, straightening the bones of paralytics and setting them on their feet, casting out demons, giving sight to the blind, raising the dead, and even more. He wants these signs to serve as an example to unbelievers so that they can experience the power and authority of God displayed in believers. This is clear in Acts 13:9–12, when the apostle Paul is in Cyprus and the sorcerer Bar-Jesus or Elymus tries to prevent the proconsul Sergius Paulus from hearing Paul and Barnabas talk about the Word of God.

> Then Saul, who was also called Paul, filled with the Holy Spirit, looked straight at Elymas and said, "You are a child of the devil and an enemy of everything that is right! You are full of all kinds of deceit and trickery. Will you never stop perverting the right ways of the

> Lord? Now the hand of the Lord is against you. You are going to be blind for a time, not even able to see the light of the sun." Immediately mist and darkness came over him, and he groped about, seeking someone to lead him by the hand. **When the proconsul saw what had happened, he believed, for he was amazed at the teaching about the Lord**. (Acts 13:9-12).

In Exodus 9:16, the Lord God clearly announces His purpose in showing His power through Moses.

> But **I have raised you up for this very purpose, that I might show you my power and that my name might be proclaimed in all the earth**. (Exodus 9:16).

When believers tell unbelievers that God loves them and wants the best for them, the ideal and advisable thing for them to do is demonstrate it by using God's power to heal, settle peace in their hearts, return their eyesight, cast out demons, and more. When unbelievers see that this evidence confirms that God truly love them, they will most likely want to live under the protection of this merciful God.

The problem is that nowadays because most believers have not activated the power or authority that God has for and holds out to them, it is very difficult for God to use them to express His love for others. Worse yet, many believers do not even have the things that the Lord provides as an extra bonus when they join God's kingdom. These added things generally involve well-being, material abundance, or other similar benefits that hold little weight in the spiritual world.

It is worth remembering that God's great servants, such as Abraham, Isaac, Jacob, Job, David, and Solomon, were naturally prosperous because God blessed them with abundant material wealth. In fact, the wealthiest figures in the Old Testament were believers and great servants of God.

The text clearly says in the following passage where Abraham sent his servant to find a wife for his son Isaac in Genesis 24:34–35.

> "So he said, 'I am Abraham's servant. **The Lord has blessed my master abundantly, and he has become wealthy. He has given him sheep and cattle, silver and gold, male and female servants, and camels and donkeys.**" (Genesis 24:34-35).

God also wishes for entire people groups to prosper. All they need to do is obey Him and follow His tenets and precepts. We see this in Joshua 22:8, when the armies made of the families of Ruben, Gad, and the half-tribe of Manasseh returned to their land across the Jordan after helping their sister tribes conquer the land God had given them.

> Then Joshua blessed them and sent them away … saying, "**Return to your homes with your great wealth**—with large herds of livestock, with silver, gold, bronze and iron, and a great quantity of clothing—and divide the plunder from your enemies with your fellow Israelites." (Joshua 22:8).

Today, however, we see many believers leading spare, straitened lives, which lack material things, because even though they are children of God, paradoxically, they all too often do not believe their Father God. This constrains the Lord from blessing them in everything, as He would like to do.

When unbelievers see that believers have nothing substantial that gives a witness of their faith in God—no power, authority, or material wealth because they are materially poor—they fail to consider this as a model for their own lives. They may even lose all respect for such believers.

This is why it is incumbent on all believers to activate, develop, and avail themselves of their power and authority. A believer without power or authority is of very little use in the kingdom of God on Earth. As members of God's mighty army, believers have a mission, which is to fight evil and help enthrone the good. They need His power to be the Lord's witnesses on Earth. Jesus says this in Acts 1:8, when He announces what is to come on Pentecost.

> But you will receive power when the Holy Spirit comes on you; **and you will be my witnesses in Jerusalem, and in all Judea and Samaria, and to the ends of the earth**. (Acts 1:8).

Ultimately, the reasons that God puts His power and authority in His believers is for many to marvel at Him, believe that He truly exists, and enlist in the army of this conquering, wonder-working God. There is a passage in Acts 9:34–35 where Peter arrives in Lydda and heals Aeneas, who had been a bedridden paralytic for eight years.

> "Aeneas," Peter said to him, "Jesus Christ heals you. Get up and roll up your mat." Immediately Aeneas got up. All those who lived in Lydda and Sharon saw him **and turned to the Lord**. (Acts 9:34-35).

Clearly, the unbelievers who saw God's miracles wrought through the believers—in this case Peter—not only marveled but also turned to the Lord and signed up for His army. It is still crucial today for modern believers to let God's power shine forth in their lives so that they can work signs, wonders, and miracles.

Materialistic humanism, however, has wreaked great havoc in human lives today and even penetrated the hearts of many believers. This has led them to think and act in the flesh and trust in their natural senses instead of battling in the spirit and trusting their spiritual senses. Believers must seek to activate their spiritual senses and diligently use them to develop the power that the Lord has placed within their reach. They also need to stop leaning so much on their natural senses, which too often, betray and deceive us, and cannot be trusted. Remember that our natural senses were activated only after the first humans sinned and were degraded, ceasing to be a spiritual essence and becoming a natural essence.

Finally, believers must seek to live an upright life, with strength and joy in our hearts regardless of the circumstances of life. Whatever happens, we will always have troubles, face difficulties, and come up against obstacles in our paths, trip, and fall. We must always keep uppermost the knowledge that our strength comes from God. When others—especially unbelievers—see our attitudes, assurances, and upright, joy-filled lives, they will admire us and want the same thing for their own lives. This is one of the best ways to serve and honor the Lord our God.

Chapter 12

GOD'S TRIPLE CO-INHERENCY OR TRINITARIAN CO-INHERENCY

We have already defined co-inherency or cohabitation as a mutual dwelling between two entities. In this case, it is between God's Holy Spirit and the human soul. Both simultaneously dwell one in the other and in perfect fellowship and harmony. As such, triple co-inherency or cohabitation is the mutual indwelling among three entities. Each one simultaneously dwells inside the other two and in perfect fellowship and harmony.

12.1. God's Triple Co-Inherency

Perfect co-inherency exists between God the Father, God the Son, and God the Holy Spirit.

This co-inherency or cohabitation among the three persons of the Holy Trinity is called, the triple co-inherency or the Trinitarian co-inherency of God. This means that at all time, the fullness of each of the three persons and of God himself are simultaneously present within each of the other two persons of the divine Trinity.

John 14:8–11 describes the co-inherency between the Father and the Son as follows:

> Philip said, "Lord, show us the Father and that will be enough for us." Jesus answered, "Don't you know me, Philip, even after I have been among you such a long time? Anyone who has seen me has seen the Father. How can you say, 'Show us the Father'? Don't you believe that I am in the Father, and that the Father is in me? The words I say to you I do not speak on my own authority. Rather, it is the Father, living in me, who is doing His work. **Believe me when I say that I am in the Father and the Father is in me**; or at least believe on the evidence of the works themselves. (John 14:8-11).

Thus, the Holy Trinity or God the one in three is always present in each of His three persons.

Sometimes God the Father takes precedence or moves into action. At other times, God the Son does this, and in others, God the Holy Spirit does this. Even so, in all cases, the three persons of God one in three are together. God's Trinitarian co-inherency is unchanging.

All this further demonstrates that the three persons of the holy Trinity always work together. This is of uppermost importance because neither the Father, nor the Son, nor the

Holy Spirit ever acts alone, but they are always together and always work together.

We have been taught that God is present in His three persons. This is true because, God in His three persons is ever and always present simultaneously in each one of them. This was explained earlier in the discussion on the Hologram Principle. The triple co-inherency or triple cohabitation of God was established in God the Alpha at the very beginning.

12.2. The Triple Co-Inherency of the Soul

When God created humankind, as it was said early on, He made people with a special spiritual essence that was different from His own essence. He created them with the spiritual essence known as their soul, which He also created as a trinity of mind, emotions, and will, in a triple co-inherency or triple cohabitation. This means that the human mind exists in co-inherency with the emotions, the emotions exist in co-inherency with the will, and the will exists in co-inherency with the mind. It also means that the fullness of each one of the three parts of the soul—mind, emotions, and will—and the soul itself are simultaneously and always present within all the other parts or essences of the soul.

This relationship of co-inherency or cohabitation within the trinity of the human soul is called, triple co-inherency of the soul, or Trinitarian co-inherency of the soul. It explains why our thoughts (mind), our feelings (emotions), and our decisions (will) are all interconnected. These essences all work together within the human soul.

There are times when the soul-mind takes precedence or action. In other cases, it is the soul-emotions. In others, it is the soul-will. In all these cases, the three parts are together, and the Trinitarian co-inherency of the human soul is unchanging.

12.3. The Triple Co-Inherency of God and His Family or of the Omega God

God's will, is to be in triple co-inherency with His family, both His bride and His children. God's plan before the founding of the world was to set himself up in triple co-inherency with His family, which, as we have seen, is God's purpose for all creation. He wants to found His family and build His lineage.

Therefore, the Lord, God the Father, will be in co-inherency with His children, the believers. His children will be in co-inherency with their mother, the holy church or the bride of the Lamb. The bride, in turn, will be in co-inherency with her bridegroom, the Father. This triple co-inherency of God's family is called, the triple co-inherency of the Omega God. Remember that in the end, the Omega God will be alone as God, but He will have been "made larger" by His family, which will be part of Him. Moreover, we saw under the Inverse Hologram Principle that because the Spirit of God is in co-inherency with the souls of believers, once they have departed from this world, the Holy Spirit (the piece of God's hologram) would return to be with God and take the souls of believers back with Him.

The triple co-inherency of God's family or the Trinitarian co-inherency of God´s family; is being established, as He forms His family or His holy dwelling place. For all eternity, God will be in perfect fellowship and harmony, dwelling in His children and His bride (the bride of the Lamb or the church), which is the mother of His children. They, in turn, will be in perfect harmony, dwelling in God and His bride (their mother or the holy church). Finally, His bride will dwell in perfect harmony with God the Father and in His children. All of them together will become the New Jerusalem, the heart of God, His holy dwelling place, and the home of His children.

12.4. The Super Hologram of God and the Super Hologram of the Universe

We have seen that when God made plans to build His family, He did not want to force His people to love and accept him, so He created them with free will. Then to ensure their full freedom to exercise their will, God created a parallel reality, which was very different from His own. It was an infinite natural reality. God created the universe. He created it with great complexity and all the features that were necessary for it to be a sufficiently attractive reality, which could become an alternative for the exercise of human free will. Thus, God created the universe to be astounding, imposing, majestic, and infinite, to underscore His own grandeur and represent a visible reality in contrast to himself, an invisible reality.

He created a type of physical or natural replica of the spiritual universe or the kingdom of God. On the physical plane, the universe is a type of sample or visible representation of the kingdom of God. It is especially, geared to stand as a witness to the grandeur and immensity of God. He created the universe with a full array of features that are similar to His own kingdom, but He also created it with other qualities, that are diametrically opposed to His own essence.

By extension, if God is a sort of super hologram, the super hologram of God, the universe can be seen as, a super hologram of the universe. Both represent holograms of infinite dimensions, one in the spiritual realm, and the other in the natural.

It is instructive to look at some of the qualities that the spiritual universe of God has in common with the physical or natural universe that He created.

1. Both possess the functionality of a type of super hologram.
2. Both are immense and majestic.
3. Both are infinite.
4. Natural elements existing in the physical universe (Earth), such as water, rock, gold, silver, precious stones, blood, light, wood, and the like are physical replicas of the same elements that first existed and still exist in the spiritual universe or the kingdom of God.

Remember that God showed Moses the models that exist in heaven so that he could copy them and build their natural replicas on Earth. This is addressed in Exodus 25:37–40 and 26:30.

> Then make its seven lamps and set them up on it so that they light the space in front of it. Its wick trimmers and trays are to be of pure gold. A talent of pure gold is to be used for the lampstand and all these accessories. **See that you make them according to the pattern shown you on the mountain**. (Exodus 25:37–40).

> Set up the tabernacle **according to the plan shown you on the mountain**. (Exodus 26:30).

The next example is from Revelation 21:18–21, when John was taken to heaven, and was shown the events of the Last Times.

> **The wall was made of jasper, and the city of pure gold**, as pure as glass. **The foundations of the city walls were decorated with every kind of precious stone**. The first foundation was jasper, the second sapphire, the third agate, the fourth emerald, the fifth onyx, the sixth ruby, the seventh chrysolite, the eighth beryl, the ninth topaz, the tenth turquoise, the eleventh jacinth, and the twelfth amethyst. **The twelve gates were twelve pearls**, each gate made of a single pearl. The great street of the city was of gold, as pure as transparent glass. (Revelation 21:18-21).

The precious stones and gold were not natural or physical like those on Earth. They were spiritual, as in the kingdom of God where everything is spiritual.

Now we can examine just a few of the contrasts between the kingdom of God or super hologram of God and the universe or super hologram of the universe.

1. The universe is physical or natural while the kingdom of God is spiritual.
2. The universe is visible and in general, perceptible with the natural senses while the kingdom of God is invisible, and therefore, it is perceptible only by human supra-senses or spiritual senses.
3. The universe is temporary while the kingdom of God is everlasting.
4. The universe was created, while the kingdom of God was not created. It has always been.

When God created humankind, He made people in His own image and likeness in the spiritual sense while on the material or physical plane; He created them in the image and likeness of the universe. With the fall of humankind, people lost their image and likeness of God—the spiritual image of God—but retained the physical, earthly image and likeness of the universe.

1st. Corinthians 15:49 shows how humankind was created in a dual image.

> And just as we have borne **the image of the earthly man**, so shall we bear **the image of the heavenly man**. (1st. Corinthians 15:49).

This means that when you were first born, you were born as a piece of the universe's hologram, but you were lacking the piece of God's hologram. Your body belongs to the super hologram of the universe. We know that when you, as a human being, receive the Holy Spirit, you acquire the image and likeness of God and begin to belong to the super hologram of God.

People who depart from this world not having received Jesus Christ as Lord and Savior—therefore, not having received a piece God's hologram are not children of God. Thus, under the Inverse Hologram Principle, their physical body returns to the super hologram of the universe, which in this particular case means that it returns to Earth. Their souls, which remain spiritually dead because they have not received the Spirit of God or the piece God's hologram, which, as we saw, is a sort of admission ticket or passport, remains dead for all eternity, and therefore, forever separate from God.

However, when believers who have a piece of God's hologram depart from this world, the concepts that we have now learned apply doubly because under the Inverse Hologram Principle, their physical bodies return to the super hologram of the universe. This means that they return to Earth while the piece God's hologram returns with the believers' souls to the super hologram of God, or the kingdom of God. As we have already seen, the Holy Spirit acts as a sort of admission ticket or passport that God offers to us so that we can travel, enter His kingdom, and enjoy eternal life. In Ecclesiastes 12:7, this process is described as follows:

> ...**and the dust returns to the ground it came from, and the spirit returns to God who gave it**. (Ecclesiastes 12:7).

At the same time, because we, in our physical or natural state, are a piece of the universe's hologram, the totality of the universe's expression is within us. This is because of the Hologram Principle.

In short, God created us with the potential to be part of two worlds or super holograms. As part of the super hologram of the universe, He created us with one part that is physical or natural, equipping us with natural senses. As part of the super hologram of God, the other part is spiritual. For this purpose, the Lord endowed us with supra-senses or spiritual senses. He did all this so that we could play out our lives in both worlds. Hereby, we can exercise our free will to choose our own paths and ultimately, our final destiny.

12.5. Is the Universe Simply an Illusion? Is It a Ghost?

It seems paradoxical that human beings tend to classify ghosts as spiritual beings or ones that come from the spiritual world and that are invisible to us with our natural eyes. Meanwhile, what is truly phantasmagorical is the universe itself and everything in it. The reason for this is that the universe is only an apparition because it does not exist from the spiritual standpoint, which is the reality and the true dimension in which everything that exists can be found. The universe does not exist in the reality of eternity.

In fact, the spiritual world is the real world because it is eternal. Thus, the universe is an apparition, a huge ghost. Things that are naturally visible are themselves ghosts or apparitions. In the same way that they came into being during creation, they will disappear at the end, because, they are passing, and not eternal. They belong to a time-bound reality.

This is why the universe is an enormous illusion, a gigantic and phantasmagorical hologram, which God created within the natural or physical reality as part of His plan. His purpose was to provide His people with a natural alternative to God's spiritual offering, which is real. He did this so that we could exercise our free will to choose between one reality and the other.

God wanted physical or natural reality to be as attractive and real for people as it could be so that they could exercise their free will as impartially as possible. This claim that the universe does not exist within eternal reality is evidence-based. Specifically, once God finishes building His family—his bride and children—and building His holy dwelling place—the New Jerusalem—heaven and Earth (the universe) will cease to exist. The Lord underscores the temporary nature of the universe in Matthew 24:35 and Luke 12:33.

> **Heaven and earth will pass away**, but my words will never pass away. (Matthew 24:35, Luke 12:33).

The temporary status of the universe is emphasized again in 2nd Corinthians 4:18 and Revelation 21:1.

> So we fix our eyes not on what is seen, but on what is unseen, since **what is seen is temporary, but what is unseen is eternal**. (2nd Corinthians 4:18).

> Then **I saw "a new heaven and a new earth," for the first heaven and the first earth had passed away**, and there was no longer any sea. (Revelation 21:1).

God is truly astonishing! He created an entire majestic universe that was full of wonders and infinite in its natural state so that we could have access to another option, an alternative to God. Because this alternative is the antithesis of God, it guarantees that we are truly able to exercise our own free will. As a result, many people while using their freedom, choose creation or the universe over its creator. They choose a ghost instead of reality.

12.6. The Link or Convergence between the Natural World and the Spiritual World

In view of what we know about the nature of each one, it seems irrational, nonsensical, a great trifle and even unbalanced to talk about a link or convergence between the natural or physical world and the spiritual world. Even so, we know that everything is possible with God.

On the other hand, we know the human skull contains his brain. Less obvious for many is the notion that the brain contains the human heart, and the heart contains the soul. Actually, everything resides and happens inside the human head. The brain is one of God's great masterworks, because it contains the only place in creation that is capable of allowing a special fellowship, a transition, a link, or convergence between the spiritual world and the natural world. Between the super hologram of God and the super hologram of the universe, that is, between the kingdom of God and the universe.

The soul is the contact point in this transition, and more specifically, this contact point is the human faith. Faith is an attribute of the human soul. It is a bridge between the natural and the spiritual. It is the only place where a transition or link occurs, a convergence between the natural and the spiritual world or the two mutually exclusive super holograms, because the natural world is 100% physical and 0% spiritual, while the spiritual world is 0% physical or natural and 100% spiritual.

Even so, through the human's brain, within their hearts, specifically in their souls, through faith, there is a kind of miraculous link between both "worlds", that is, between both super-holograms. Expressed in mathematical terms, would be that that the two worlds "intersect" each other in the faith of the human soul, producing a sort of "coexistence" between the two.

As discussed earlier, the infinite infrastructure or coupling station that is lodged in every human heart is where the Holy Spirit can hitch himself to us and dwell within our hearts.

This is part of the logistics, that allows the process of transition, and linkage between the two worlds.

It is known that the control panel of connections or circuits in the human brain is infinite, an appropriate and exact condition to facilitate the coupling of an infinite being, which is precisely God, by means of His Holy Spirit.

12.6.1. Faith, Human Time, and God's Time

Human beings live in the natural world, somewhere between past and future, between that which was and that which is not yet. The present is nothing but an illusion because when the future approaches the present, it slips away, disappears and becomes the past.

God is different. Unlike ourselves, who have no present, God is and remains in an eternal present, where there is neither past nor future. In God's kingdom, what has passed and what is still to come already are. His eternity is a present time where all things are—those that have been and those that have not yet been. It is truly extraordinary to our eyes.

This present time that approaches us, slips away, and immediately jumps from the future into the past, is the very same stable, eternal condition where God resides. Thus, the kingdom of God exists outside of time.

It would appear that King Solomon had a premonition of this condition when he said the following in Ecclesiastes 3:14–15:

> I know that everything God does will endure forever; nothing can be added to it and nothing taken from it. God does it so that people will fear him. **Whatever is has already been, and what will be has been before**; and God will call the past to account. (Ecclesiastes 3:14-15).

Nonetheless, although it is true that we live in a world that skips from the future into the past without touching the present (because just like the hands of a clock, time never stops in the present), we are able to gain access to God's eternal present tense by means of our faith.

It is faith that can penetrate God's eternal present or eternity and transfer human beings into the present, which forever and always has been the time of the kingdom of God. Faith is the only key that is able to open the door to eternity and give us access to God's present tense. We have no access to it except by faith.

Faith, then, is akin to a time machine, by which we humans can cross the time barrier, reach eternity, and become attuned to it. This is one of God's wonders!

Clearly, the great blessings that God has for us, alongside salvation itself, exist in God's eternal present tense. All we have to do is, use our time machine, our faith, enter into this present tense, become attuned to eternity, and reach out for all God´s blessings. This is not a fairy tale but a true time machine to our disposal: Our faith.

Finally, there is a paradox to consider. The past and future, between which we live out our natural lives, ultimately do not exist. The past has already happened, and the future will never arrive. Because they are slippery and unstable, neither the past nor the future, can be relied on. The paradox is that the present, which is but an illusion for the natural person, is the only time dimension that is truly stable and reliable. If we are to enter into this present tense, however, we need to experience transmutation from our natural, current status to a new spiritual status. We can build our own time machine by building up and strengthening our faith.

12.6.2. One More Thought about Time

Time is a gift given by God. The time we know on Earth, though, is a strictly limited good or asset. This makes it far more valuable than silver and gold. You can always work harder to increase your material holdings, but nothing you can do to obtain more time. This is why you must invest the time you have with the greatest of care and wisdom. The best business you can ever undertake with your time is drawing nearer to God. Because, as you become closer to God, you are also closer to the eternal life that exists only in Him. This eternal life will give you unlimited time. This means that if you take the limited time that is available to you in this world and invest it in God, you will gain access to the unlimited time that is in the kingdom of God, that is, in God himself.

12.7. Jesus Christ: The Firstborn among the Dead

Before the death and resurrection of Jesus Christ, no one had ever risen with a glorified body. Jesus was the firstborn among the dead, because He was the first child of God among the children of men to have departed from this world and gone to the bosom of God. This is why He is also the head or cornerstone of the church. He is the first living, precious stone in God's house. Colossians 1:18 says it like this:

> And **He is the head of the body, the church; He is the beginning, the firstborn from among the dead**, so that in everything He might have the supremacy. (Colossians 1:18).

Jesus Christ, as the firstborn of God, became the head of the body of Christ (the temple of God) and the cornerstone of the house of God. This house is alive, under construction, and in constant growth. We see it in Ephesians 2:20–22.

> …, built on the foundation of the apostles and prophets, **with Christ Jesus himself as the chief cornerstone**. In him the whole building is joined together and rises to become a holy temple in the Lord. And in him you too are being built together to become a dwelling in which God lives by his Spirit. (Ephesians 2:20-22).

12.8. The Primary Receiving Channel (PRC) and the Secondary Receiving Channel (SRC) of Jesus Christ

Both of Jesus's primary and secondary receiving channels were fully developed. As a man, He received all communications from the Farther over his primary receiving channel (PRC) while over his secondary receiving channel (SRC), He was able to hear or perceive all the thoughts of other people and spiritual beings. This is clear in the Bible in the texts of Luke 6:7–8 and 11:17. Luke 6:7-8 is a passage in which Jesus was teaching in the synagogue on the day of rest. A man who was there had a withered right hand. It says,

> The Pharisees and the teachers of the law were looking for a reason to accuse Jesus, so they watched him closely to see if He would heal on the Sabbath. **But Jesus knew what they were thinking** and said to the man with the shriveled hand, "Get up and stand in front of everyone." So he got up and stood there. (Luke 6:7-8).

Luke 11:17 tells the story of Jesus expelling a demon, after which the mute man began to speak. The people were astonished, and some said that Jesus expelled demons by the power of Beelzebub, the prince of demons.

> **Jesus knew their thoughts** and said to them: "Any kingdom divided against itself will be ruined, and a house divided against itself will fall." (Luke 11:17).

In these and many other passages from the Word, it is clear that Jesus knew what people were thinking. This is because His SRC was so fully developed.

Chapter 13

SPECIAL NUGGETS

This chapter summarizes a variety of facts or truths intended to instruct, clarify, and reinforce concepts of general interest. These nuggets are not necessarily related to one and other. However, they do serve a common purpose, which is to underscore certain essential facts that may help enhance your understanding of the character of God.

13.1. Nugget Number One: From Love and Obedience to Sacrifice, and from Sacrifice to Love and Obedience

Before the fall, Adam and Eve lived in obedience, fellowship, and perfect love with God. This era is called the pre-sin period (prior to human sinfulness). No blood sacrifice was needed at that time because there was no sin to atone for, and no one held any sin. All that was needed was to express their love for God by obeying Him. Much to our own sorrow, we all know that they failed at it and disobeyed God. Love and obedience were the very foundation of the relationship that was between God and His people (Adam and Eve) during the pre-sin period.

As we have already seen, after the fall of Adam and Eve, sin corrupted the human heart, and evil took over the human soul, and consequently, distanced them from God, their Creator. Since that time, God's wrath has constantly been inflamed against His people. God separated himself from them, and they became strangers to Him. The only way for them to soothe His wrath and temporarily approach Him was by offering endless, interminable blood sacrifices to atone for their sins, which were many and frequent. Human evil blocked love, the very essence of God, from reaching them the way that He would have wished.

That is why, during the period that spans from the fall of Adam and Eve to the death and resurrection of Jesus Christ, the relationship between God and His people was characterized by sacrifice rather than love through obedience. Therefore, it became necessary and crucial to eliminate sin from the human heart and to restore and reestablish our relationship with God, according to the original plans and purposes that He had for us.

Under this setting and these circumstances, God sent His Son to perform the final sacrifice, which would redeem us once, and for all from sin and death. By cleansing sin from the human heart, God could restart the relationship of love and enter into perfect fellowship with us. After Jesus

Christ's blood was shed completing the ultimate sacrifice, the prevailing relationship between God and His people became once again one of love and obedience.

Having completed the final sacrifice of Jesus Christ, God opens the door for us to go back in time to a condition that was similar to the pre-sin era of Adam and Eve. Now our only duty is devoting ourselves to loving and obeying Him. Today, we must emphasize God's love above all things. This explains why Jesus Christ gave us only two commandments. The first is to love God with all our heart, soul, mind, and strength. The second is to love our neighbors as ourselves.

The Ten Commandments served the purpose of preventing people from sinning. The purpose of these two commandments is to set up a triangle of perfect love between God the Father, the bride of the Lamb (church of Christ), and His children (all those who are saved in Christ).

In short, the relationship between God and humankind from the time He created Adam and Eve until their fall was marked by love and obedience. Afterward, that relationship would be based on sacrifices, a period that spans from the fall of Adam and Eve until the death and resurrection of Jesus Christ. Finally, we returned to a new era of love and obedience that began with the death and resurrection of

Jesus Christ, and it will last until the end of this world, when God will fulfill His purpose of building a family.

The Lord ordered us to love Him with all our heart, soul, mind, and strength. That love should be expressed in the form of obedience, where we turn away from sin and always do God's will. We must not forget that our present days on Earth are part of the era of love and obedience that God expects from all of us.

13.2. Nugget Number Two: Our God-Given Primary Source of Energy

There is no question that God set the sun in place as our primary source of energy. We know that all forms of life on Earth can exist only because of the sun and consequently, solar energy. All other forms of energy that are available to us today, whether hydrocarbons, water power, atomic energy, geothermal energy, biomass, or wind, originated in the same essential source—the sun. There is a paradox in this. With the surge in technological developments over the past one hundred years, we have practically turned our backs on the sun, not taking in account that it is the very source of energy that God gave us to exploit and use to meet all our needs.

The sun, as the first and primary source of energy for our planet, is still there. It is ready for us to start developing it extensively. It can make our lives on Earth easier for the following fundamental reasons:

1. Solar energy comes from a source that will remain inexhaustible as long as we live in this world.
2. It is the most renewable of all the renewable energies on Earth.
3. It is the cleanest energy source and truly pollution-free.
4. It is the most available and affordable source that we have.

Despite all this, humankind has made very limited use of the sun as a major source of energy. Instead, we have mostly drawn from derivative, secondary sources, especially hydrocarbons. We have turned the world's human population into an oil-centrist society, which revolves almost entirely around hydrocarbons—especially oil—as the major source that meets our needs.

We have gotten ourselves stuck in a trap by placing hydrocarbon-based energy at the center of human development, ignoring God's will and His best intentions.

1. The sun does not pollute because it is entirely harmless to the environment, but hydrocarbons are one of the most contaminating, destructive sources of energy in use today. Think of the many tragedies

that have been caused by oil tankers poisoning billions of gallons of ocean water and immeasurable miles of beaches and killing countless land and sea creatures. Add to this the worst oil disaster in history, when millions of barrels of petroleum leaked out of control into the Gulf of Mexico.

2. The sun is an inexhaustible source of energy, but hydrocarbon resources are finite.
3. Hydrocarbons, in general terms, poison and contaminate human society, land, water, aquatic species, and the atmosphere. They inflict severe damage on the planet, but the sun purifies the air and revives the earth because it is a natural source of life.
4. Hydrocarbons are not a freely available source of energy. Not everyone has access to them because they are owned by a small group of nations while, the sun is universally available.
5. Hydrocarbons come up from the very bowels of the earth, and generally, they can be described as an agent of death. Solar energy comes from the heavens, and it is an agent, that preserves and maintains life.
6. The Sun was created by God, as a blessing and as a mean of feeding life on Earth. Hydrocarbons are more of a curse because they are dug up to

scatter evil throughout the planet in the form of poison, death, pollution, hunger, exploitation, marginalization, exclusion, hatred, persecution, war, and more.

People have always underrated the sun as a major source of energy. Thus, they have not taken the time, relied on God, and invested enough resources to investigate, discover, and develop the technology that is necessary to bring about the universal and efficient use of solar energy.

At creation, God placed on the Earth, all the material that we needed to develop new combinations and the right technologies to tap into the sun's energy for all our uses and needs. Today, He is still waiting for us to take the step of faith that is necessary for Him to help us develop this technology broadly and fully.

If we ever take an interest in developing true solar-based-energy technology, our energy future will be fully guaranteed, and we will finally come into alignment with God's will, as far as energy is concerned.

Indeed, as I complete the final review of this manuscript for publication, I must say that the progress made in recent years in research and development of solar energy has been remarkable. It would appear that we have finally decided to seriously, move in the direction of technological development for solar energy, especially for electricity.

It took us until late in the first decade of the twenty-first century to start making it commercially competitive. At the current pace of technological progress, it seems reasonable to expect that in only a few more years, solar energy will take its place at the top of the charts as a source for generating the world's electricity—at last!

13.3. Nugget Number Three: The Rich and the Poor in God's Eyes

It is not a sin to be wealthy. It is quite the contrary. God desires for all His children to prosper in everything, and of course, this includes material well-being.

After all, God is the owner of all wealth. He wishes to share it with all His children. What God hates is when people give primacy to material goods and wealth, over and above himself. We see this in 1st. John 2:15–17.

> **Do not love the world or anything in the world. If anyone loves the world, love for the Father is not in them**. For everything in the world—the lust of the flesh, the lust of the eyes, and the pride of life—comes not from the Father but from the world. The world and its desires pass away, but whoever does the will of God lives forever. (1st. John 2:15-17).

The problem is that wealth and material goods often become a great distraction for us and distance us from God, because of our tendency to make them our idols and start believing that we don't need God. It is a trap because earthly goods then become a distraction and push us away from what really matters, which is God. This is why riches so often make their owners foolish, irrational, and insensitive. Their insensitivity is particularly acute with regard to their spiritual senses, and they end up hardening their hearts and turning their backs on God. The fact is that if you do not have God, you have nothing.

The case of the poor is different. Having no material goods or very few of them, they are less prone to become distracted by them. As they do not need to fret about their wealth and their goods, they instead tend to grow closer to God and seek His favor and protection. Some become nearly desperate in their pursuit of God and cling to Him out of need because of their lack of material goods. Even though this poverty-driven need is what pushes them closer to God, they find favor in His sight, and the Lord creates the opportunity to minister to their hearts, which are not so distracted or trapped by earthly goods.

Of course, there are exceptions because we have also seen many poor people who allow themselves to become contaminated by their overwhelming desire to acquire wealth, and too often, this pushes them to the brink of envy and greed. By, the same token wealth leads some people to exercise their free wills, turn away from God, reject Him, or choose the world. By contrast, many poor people exercise that same free will out of their poverty, choose God, submit to Him, love Him, and obey Him. Others who are wealthy devote much of their time and treasure to working for God and helping and serving the poor. There are many exceptions on both sides.

In summary, those who are wealthy in earthly goods tend to be poor in faith while those who are poor in earthly goods tend to be wealthy in faith. James 2:5 explains it like this:

> Listen, my dear brothers and sisters: **Has not God chosen those who are poor in the eyes of the world to be rich in faith** and to inherit the kingdom He promised those who love him? (James 2:5).

How it would please the Lord if those who are wealthy in earthly goods were counted as poor before God, seeking Him with all their hearts, and achieving true wealth! This is wealth in faith—spiritual wealth—the only one that leads to eternal life.

Such a dichotomy between rich and poor does not need to be like this. Indeed, it is not the case for many who, although wealthy in earthly goods, have understood that true wealth lies in the love for God. Unfortunately, today the former situation is the rule while the latter is the exception.

In Old Testament times, material prosperity was actually the norm among the great servants of God and not the exception. Abraham, Isaac, Jacob, Joseph, Job, David, Solomon, and many others are counted among the many Bible characters who owned abundant wealth and earthly goods. At the same time, they loved God with devotion. These servants of God understood that all things are of God, by God, and for God, who is the Creator of everything. They knew that they must depend on the Lord, the Creator, the Source, the Provider, and the Owner of all. King David said it clearly in 1st. Chronicles 29:11–14. Job echoed it in Job 1:21.

> Yours, Lord, is the greatness and the power and the glory and the majesty and the splendor, **for everything in heaven and earth is yours**. Yours, Lord, is the kingdom; you are exalted as head over all. **Wealth and honor come from you; you are the ruler of all things**. In your hands are strength and power to exalt and give strength to all. Now, our God, we give you thanks, and praise your glorious name. "But who am I, and who are my people, that we should be able to give as generously as this? **Everything comes from**

> **you, and we have given you only what comes from your hand.** (1st. Chronicles 29:11–14).

> And [Job] said: "Naked I came from my mother's womb, and naked I will depart. **The Lord gave and the Lord has taken away**; may the name of the Lord be praised." (Job 1:21)

All these faithful ones knew exactly where they stood regarding wealth and material goods versus their relationship with God. Their clarity of purpose enabled them to keep their gaze fixed on their Creator and not on the creation, the way so many do today. We have much to learn from them about the primacy of God in our relationship to material things.

13.4. Nugget Number Four: Why Should Believers Congregate?

There are many reasons why it is important to congregate, and although Christians know this very well, it can never be overstated. Because there are people who would rather ignore the need to congregate, we will go over the three main arguments in favor of it.

1. The final destiny of all believers is to be together forever as part of the great, holy, royal family of God,

when all of us together will become His dwelling place. In eternity, no believer can stand apart like a lonely wolf or a lonely bird. For this reason, when believers congregate, they are rehearsing and demonstrating that they are capable of living together in fellowship and harmony, as this will be their lot for all eternity.

2. Believers need to congregate and interact with, encourage, lean on, and tolerate one another with patience, as they grow toward full spiritual maturity.
3. Jesus is delighted when a group of believers gathers in His name. He stands in their midst, ready to release His immense power and authority among them.

Matthew 18:20 clearly states this in a promise for all believers.

> For **where two or three gather in my name, there am I with them**. (Matthew 18:20).

When believers gather in harmony and come to agreement on any matter, such as praising the Lord or submitting a particular petition, under the Inverse Hologram Principle, the Holy Spirit, that is, the piece of God's hologram that dwells in each one, joins them together into a single whole, and sets up a sort of Master Spirit in their midst. This Master Spirit functions rather like a flame of fire that is lit by several candles. Their small lights join together into a larger flame, but in essence, it is still the same flame—the same Spirit of God displaying more power in their midst. Such a congregation of believers becomes in itself a sort of mini-church of Christ. It is nothing more than the Holy Spirit of God taking pleasure in the midst of His people. This union and pleasure of the Holy Spirit then produces the infilling of the Spirit, which unleashes great power in all the believers who have joined together.

Another useful comparison is to imagine several pieces of charcoal that are lit with a single flame and are kept separate, even after they are burning. Each one emits its own light and glows on its own. However, if they are put together, they will produce a powerful fire that shines much more intensely than the light of each separate piece. The same flame is burning each different piece, just as the same Holy Spirit is present in each believer. When each piece of burning coal is put together, they combine to form a great fire, which gains in intensity and power. Similarly, the very same Holy Spirit is in the heart of each believer. When they are together in harmony, He can unleash great power among them.

In short, believers must congregate because together, they fan into intensity, the light and power that are present in every one of them and glow. If they are always separated, each person will be like a piece of burning coal when it sits alone. It will eventually lose its glow and intensity and ultimately, grow cold.

13.5. Nugget Number Five: The Importance of Wisdom

Wisdom is one of the seven spirits of God. It is not a spirit that is separate from the Holy Spirit because wisdom is one of the Spirit's attributes and personifications. The seven spirits of God are identified in Isaiah 11:1–2.

> A shoot will come up from the stump of Jesse; from his roots a Branch will bear fruit. **The Spirit of the Lord will rest on him—the Spirit of wisdom and of understanding, the Spirit of counsel and of might, the Spirit of knowledge and fear** of the Lord. (Isaiah 11:1-2).

So we see that wisdom is a spirit, a personification of the Holy Spirit, very active, and hard at work. Indeed, wisdom is a speaking spirit, and it tells us specific things. Believers must seek, obtain, and handle wisdom as one of their most precious treasures. We see this in Proverbs 4:5–8 and 8:11.

> Get wisdom, get understanding; do not forget my words or turn away from them. Do not forsake wisdom, and she will protect you; love her, and she will watch over you. The beginning of wisdom is this: Get wisdom. Though it cost all you have, get understanding. **Cherish her,**

> **and she will exalt you; embrace her, and she will honor you.** (Proverbs 4:5-8).

> ...for wisdom is more precious than rubies, and nothing you desire can compare with her. (Proverbs 8:11).

In Proverbs 8:19, the spirit of wisdom speaks out directly.

> **My fruit is better than fine gold**; what I yield surpasses choice silver. (Proverbs 8:19).

We have a testimony of wisdom's great activism and assertiveness when she cries out to all people in her desire to win their love. Only if they turn to her can she, wisdom, love them in return and take delight in them. Wisdom speaks this out in Proverbs 8:4, 17, and 31.

> **To you, O people, I call out**; I raise my voice to all mankind. (Proverbs 8:4).

> **I love those who love me**, and those who seek me find me. (Proverbs 8:17).

> ...rejoicing in his whole world **and delighting in mankind**. (Proverbs 8:31).

Here is a list of benefits we can enjoy if we love, acquire, and treasure wisdom in our hearts.

1. **Wisdom and Prudence**
   Because wisdom and prudence dwell together, when believers acquire wisdom, they obtain prudence at the same time. In Proverbs 8:12, wisdom herself says it this way:

   > I, wisdom, **dwell together with prudence**; I possess knowledge and discretion. (Proverbs 8:12).

2. **Counsel, Sound Judgment, Insight, and Power**
   Wisdom comes in a full-package deal, including counsel, good judgment, and insight, which is wisdom herself and the power that is proper to her. Again in Proverbs 8:14, wisdom says,

   > **Counsel and sound judgment are mine; I have insight, I have power**. (Proverbs 8:14).

3. **Riches, Honor, and Righteousness**
   Wisdom is so astounding that she even brings riches, honor, and righteousness. Whoever seeks wisdom will also receive the other three in the same package. This is clear in Proverbs 8:18.

With me are riches and honor, enduring wealth and prosperity. (Proverbs 8:18).

4. **Inheritance and Treasure**
   Wisdom gives an inheritance to those who love her and fills them with treasure. We see this in Proverbs 8:21.

   Bestowing a rich inheritance on those who love me **and making their treasuries full**. (Proverbs 8:21).

5. **Blessing (Beatitude)**
   Wisdom assures blessing to all who heed her, wait at her gates, and keep her ways. She says so herself in Proverbs 8:32 and 34.

   Now then, my children, listen to me; **blessed are those who keep my ways**. (Proverbs 8:32).

   Blessed are those who listen to me, watching daily at my doors, waiting at my doorway. (Proverbs 8:34).

6. **Eternal Life and God's Favor**
   Finally, wisdom declares that those who find her find true life itself so that they gain God's favor and obtain eternal life. Wisdom says it herself in Proverbs 8:35.

> **For those who find me find life and receive favor from the Lord.** (Proverbs 8:35).

It becomes clear that believers absolutely must seek, find, love, and jealously guard wisdom, because it is with her and her support that they obtain eternal life in the kingdom of God.

13.5.1. How and Where Is Wisdom Found?

Wisdom, one of the seven spirits or manifestations of the Holy Spirit, is found in the Word of God. It is impossible to overestimate the importance of reading the Word of God every day—studying, examining, meditating on, and pondering it.

It is also good to remember the value of petitioning the Lord for wisdom and revelation. I will paraphrase Ephesians 1:17, which we mentioned at the beginning of this book.

> Glorious father, **give me the Spirit of wisdom** and revelation, so that I may know you better. (Ephesians 1:17).

God takes pleasure in our specific request to grant wisdom therefore He will respond and grant it to all those who, from the heart, that is, with faith, make said request. This gift, however, is always conditional on the believer's decision to take the necessary steps of faith and seek wisdom in God's Word.

Finally, remember that the most useful books of the Bible for believers to find wisdom and become wise themselves are Ecclesiastes and especially Proverbs. Both are a handbook or a type of road map to wisdom. It makes sense that this is true, because, many of the proverbs were written by King Solomon himself, the wisest man who has ever lived with the exception of Jesus. It makes sense to look for wisdom in the book written by the wisest of all men. Therefore, in general terms, we draw on the whole Bible to find wisdom, but more specifically, we focus on Proverbs and Ecclesiastes.

13.5.2. The Wise, the Simple, and the Foolish

All people fit into one of the following three categories: wise, simple, or foolish.

- **Wise**

We have already seen that wisdom is one of the seven spirits, personifications, or manifestations of the Holy Spirit. There is only one true wisdom. It is the wisdom from God. Outside of God's wisdom is human foolishness. God has given all true wisdom, directly or indirectly. Proverbs 2:6 explains it like this:

> For **the Lord gives wisdom**; from his mouth come knowledge and understanding. (Proverbs 2:6).

We can obtain true wisdom only from God. He reveals wisdom primarily through His Word. In general, believers are wise because the Holy Spirit has revealed and taught wisdom to them. This is why all believers need to study, examine, ponder, and meditate on the Word of God every day, to become ever wiser.

- **Foolish**

Foolishness is the antithesis of wisdom. A fool is anyone who is not wise or does not have the spirit of wisdom. Fools trust in their own opinions. All unbelievers are in the category of fools.

- **Simple**

All people are born in a state of death. They are also born simple-minded (naive, ignorant, or lacking experience). As their lives unfold, they become either wise or foolish. If we want wisdom to govern our lives, we need to treasure it up richly in our hearts. This is also the reason why human sons and daughters, especially the children of believers, need to be raised in the nurture and admonition of God and with broad knowledge of His Word. This way, they can make the shift from being simplemindedness to wisdom. Consequently, God's wisdom rather than human foolishness will take precedence in their lives.

13.5.3. The Importance of God's Spirit of Wisdom

As we saw before, there is no question that wisdom is a key concern for God, so much so, that wisdom is one of the seven spirits, personifications, or manifestations of His Spirit. Indeed, it was with wisdom that God made all creation. To understand how important wisdom is for God, we can examine wisdom's own words in Proverbs 8:22–30.

> The Lord brought me forth as the first of his works, before his deeds of old; I was formed long ages ago, at the very beginning, when the world came to be. When there were no watery depths, I was given birth, when there were no springs overflowing with water; before the mountains were settled in place, before the hills, I was given birth, before he made the world or its fields or any of the dust of the earth. **I was there when he set the heavens in place, when he marked out the horizon on the face of the deep, when he established the clouds above and fixed securely the fountains of the deep, when he gave the sea its boundary so the waters would not overstep his command,**

> **and when he marked out the foundations of the earth. Then I was constantly at his side**. I was filled with delight day after day, rejoicing always in his presence. (Proverbs 8:22-30).

This clear description shows how the spirit of wisdom played a leading role in accompanying God while the heavens, earth, and universe were being created. In the same way, wisdom must be our constant companion.

13.6. Nugget Number Six: Pastoral Ministry and God's Great Servants

Nowadays, many of God's servants seem uninterested in the ministerial gift of the pastorate or the shepherds of God's church. This assertion is because in recent years we have witnessed a clear shrinking of the ranks. It has almost been a stampede of the Lord's servants leaving this ministry. Some don′t like to be called pastor anymore, preferring the sobriquets apostle, prophet, or evangelist, labels that seem to have become trendy of late in the community of believers.

A sister in the faith recently told me that her spiritual leader had surpassed the level of pastor, suggesting that this was a lower tier in the ministry or of inferior rank in God's work, and that he had now attained the superior grade of apostle. So it would seem that in the community of believers, the idea is taking hold that being a pastor is a lower category of ministry and less honorable than the others. Ah, it is such ignorance!

We need to go back to Ephesians 4:11 and remember the five ministries that God established to perfect the saints and edify His church.

> So Christ himself gave the apostles, the prophets, the evangelists, the pastors and teachers. (Ephesians 4:11).

There is no sign of ranking by relative importance or levels of superiority among them because for the Lord's purposes, all are crucially important and relevant. These ministries complement one another as necessary strategies to fulfill God's purposes. We should also understand that it is the Lord, and He only, who distributed these ministerial gifts among people. He gave more than one to some.

This modern trend of disparaging the pastoral ministry as mere shepherds is paradoxical because of the transcendental position the office holds throughout the Bible. Pastoral ministry has profound spiritual qualities. The status of pastor, shepherd, and everything this ministry represents are the Lord's tools to work deeply within the hearts of many of His servants. The pastoral gift develops a full range of very special virtues and qualities in those who practice it. Among these virtues or qualities, we find love, obedience, patience, compassion, suffering, and more. The Lord values them very highly.

It should come as no surprise that so many of God's great servants in the Old Testament were shepherds or pastoral workers: Abel, the three patriarchs (Abraham, Isaac, and Jacob), Joseph, Moses, David, and Jesus himself, who started as a carpenter and not a shepherd in the natural sense, but He clearly was in the spiritual sense. Unquestionably, Jesus is the Pastor of pastors, and the Prince of pastors, He is the Good Shepherd.

> There is something very special in being a pastor and caring for the flock. There is great blessing for those who are worthy practitioners of pastoral ministry because the shepherd has the closest relationship to the sheep. He has the commitment to be there always. He stands in the gap, guides, protects, feeds, and cares for them.

13.7. Nugget Number Seven: The Word of God and Its Parables, Similes, Metaphors, Allegories, and Ironies

The Lord often speaks in parables, similes, metaphors, allegories, and even irony or satire. Such expressions appear frequently in the Word of God, both in the Old and New Testament. Today we know these expressions as literary devices. The Lord has always used them, especially after human fall into sin. These literary devices illustrate God's character and reveal mysteries and truths from His kingdom. The Holy Spirit shapes believers' abilities to understand them so that they can become object lessons to strengthen their faith. Jesus made the most frequent use of these devices during His time among us on Earth.

Note that our human understanding tends to be block when faced with such expressions, so that their natural minds are not able to understand God's Word expressed through them. If the Word of God is filled with parables, allegories, similes, metaphors, and other literary devices, even believers find themselves forced to examine, study, probe, discover, and internalize the mysteries, great qualities, and truths of the kingdom of God, because these truths are veiled from the natural mind.

Jesus himself confirms God's use of allegories when He says the following in John 16:25:

> Though I have been **speaking figuratively**, a time is coming when **I will no longer use this kind of language** but will tell you plainly about my Father. (John 16:25).

We even learn in Mark 4:10–12 and Luke 8:10 that one of the purposes of parables in the Word of God is to block unbelievers from understanding. It says,

> When He was alone, the Twelve and the others around Him asked Him about the parables. He told them, "The secret of the kingdom of God has been given to you. **But to those on the outside everything is said in parables so that, "'they may be ever seeing but never perceiving, and ever hearing but never understanding**; otherwise they might turn and be forgiven!'" (Mark 4:10–12).

> He said, "The knowledge of the secrets of the kingdom of God has been given to you, **but to others I speak in parables, so that, "'though seeing, they may not see; though hearing, they may not understand**.'" (Luke 8:10).

This makes sense because these expressions can be seen and understood only through the spiritual senses. Remember that in our natural state, our spiritual senses are obstructed, or they have atrophied.

There's more. Look at Jesus's words in Matthew 13:13–16 and John 8:47.

> This is why I speak to them in parables: "**Though seeing, they do not see; though hearing, they do not hear or understand**." In them is fulfilled the prophecy of Isaiah: "You will be ever hearing but never understanding; you will be ever seeing but never perceiving. For

> this people's heart has become calloused; they hardly hear with their ears, and they have closed their eyes. Otherwise they might see with their eyes, hear with their ears, understand with their hearts and turn, and I would heal them." But blessed are your eyes because they see, and your ears because they hear. (Matthew 13:13-16).

> **Whoever belongs to God hears what God says**. The reason you do not hear is that you do not belong to God. (John 8:47).

The Lord repeatedly used the expression "though seeing, they may not see; though hearing, they may not understand." He meant that even though people have their natural senses on alert (eyes, ears, touch, etc.); they cannot understand the parables, metaphors, similes, and allegories that appear in God's Word. Their supra-senses or spiritual senses, which are the only means for understanding such devices, are blocked.

In other cases, until the time that He chooses to reveal their meaning, even to believers, the Lord´s parables, are veiled.

It happened to His disciples. Luke 9:45 says:

> **"But they [the disciples] did not understand what this meant. It was hidden from them**, so that they did not grasp it, and they were afraid to ask Him about it. (Luke 9:45).

This is why people need to believe and seek the Lord with all their hearts. Thus, they will come to understand the mysteries of the kingdom of God. Proverbs 28:5 explains it like this:

> Evildoers do not understand what is right, **but those who seek the Lord understand it fully**. (Proverbs 28:5).

One of most mystifying metaphors in the Bible, even for many believers, is in Matthew 8:22, when Jesus was speaking to one of His disciples.

> But Jesus told him, "**Follow me, and let the dead bury their own dead**." (Matthew 8:22).

In this specific case, Jesus was telling His follower to let natural people or those who are spiritually dead take responsibility for burying their dead, who have departed from this world.

13.8. Nugget Number Eight: The Wisdom of Theologians

Theologians present one of the most interesting and revealing cases. Briefly, theology is the study of God. It should be safe to assume that theologians are the ones who know the most about God, because their profession and occupation is no less than to study God. Therefore, they are supposed to be the experts and top specialists on the subject of God. Paradoxically, this assumption is not necessarily true.

Just to clarify, many theologians are believers, but some are not. Believing theologians have received Jesus Christ as their Lord and Savior and have received the Holy Spirit, who lives with them in their hearts. They have a piece of God's hologram dwelling with them in their hearts. In addition, if they are scholars of the Word of God, and therefore, they are fearful of God and obedient to His precepts, unquestionably, they are among those who most intimately know the Lord, His character, and His purposes.

By contrast, if they have not received Jesus Christ as their Lord and Savior, and therefore, they do not have the Holy Spirit in their hearts, they are natural persons who are spiritually dead and are unable to understand the mysteries of the kingdom of God.

Accordingly, these theologians simply do theology as a job like any other. It is just a way to make a living. They are faced with a particular problem and disadvantage—the knowledge of the kingdom of God is veiled to them so that they can't be experts on the subject of God. Although they may be able to rattle off the concepts that they have acquired and learned, their hearts are dead, in darkness, and without knowledge, discernment, or understanding. Despite their vast intellectual accomplishments, they do not necessarily have spiritual understanding. Again, there are theologians who have not received the Lord as their Savior, and therefore, they are unbelievers.

13.9. Nugget Number Nine: A God of Variety and Diversity

Jehovah is a God of variety and great diversity. His endless creativity and ability to innovate brings a uniqueness to everything that He makes. Paradoxically, of all God's great qualities and attributes, this is probably the less valued and appreciated.

When God made the universe, He filled it with an immeasurable variety and diversity of heavenly bodies. He populated the earth with a vast variety and diversity of species, both in the plant and in the animal kingdom, from microscopic life all the way to the largest, most astonishing beasts. He then created the man and the woman, the masterpieces of all His creation. Some were black, white, yellow and brown, tall, short, in-between, and so much more. However, above all and more spectacular and impressive than anything else, He made each one unique and unrepeatable.

Even so, instead of valuing and appreciating God's infinite creativity, we have often used it to despise and reject anything different from ourselves or unfamiliar to us. We do not even consider that everything is part of God's creation and that when we despise, reject, marginalize, or exclude any part of His making, in fact, we are despising, rejecting, marginalizing, or excluding God himself, the one who made all things according to His infinite creativity and sovereign will. Therefore, no human being can legitimately proclaim love for God while disdaining and despising part of His creation.

Many believers live out their entire lives discriminating against, despising, marginalizing, excluding, or oppressing other people and even other believers, ignoring the fact that the people they so despise are part of God's masterpiece of creation. He is a God who shows no favoritism, but instead, He orders us all to love our neighbors as ourselves.

13.9.1. When We Show Favoritism among Others, We Interfere with God

Believers must take great care not to interfere with God. Many people, including believers, show favoritism, even though the Lord clearly admonishes us not to do so. Why doesn't the Lord want believers to show favoritism? What does favoritism really mean? Showing favoritism means discriminating against certain people and even marginalizing them in deference to others. It means unfairly placing some above others and extending unjustified preferences for some people over others.

Always remember that every single person is a masterpiece of God's creation. He does not allow us, whether directly or indirectly, to discriminate against any of His creatures. Even so, too many believers disobey God's commandment and regularly discriminate against certain people, including other believers, who are their brothers and sisters.

The fact is that believers must not merely accept but actively delight in the differences that God created among people, even though, the world enjoys demonizing these differences. Believers should, at least tolerate differences in color, language, ethnic origin, culture, nationality, and so much more. The only difference that we should ever draw among others is between those who belong to Christ and those who do not. Even with this difference, believers must show mercy to those who do not belong to Christ and make a sincere effort to evangelize and win them for Christ.

When believers show favoritism among others, they run the risk of interfering with God's work and hindering God. This is very clear in a story from the book of Acts, when Peter and most of the apostles had shown favoritism among others because they did not agree that the gospel could be for Gentiles as well as Jews. They held onto this conviction even though the Lord himself had given orders to the contrary when Peter went to Caesarea to visit Cornelius. Acts 10:34–35 and 11:17 tell the story as follows:

> Then Peter began to speak: "I now realize how true it is that **God does not show favoritism** but accepts from every nation the one who fears him and does what is right. (Acts 10:34-35).
>
> So if God gave them the same gift he gave us who believed in the Lord Jesus Christ, **who was I to think that I could stand in God's way**?" (Acts 11:17).

Christians must never forget that God through His Holy Spirit have conceived those who received Jesus Christ as Lord and Savior. Therefore, they are children of God, and consequently, they are our brothers or sisters, and part of God's great family. Details such as color, ethnicity, culture, and nationality have no part in this, nor do physical or natural traits. As we said before, the Lord is a God of variety and diversity, and His sons and daughters come in all imaginable colors and flavors. Also, remember that in our final form, believers will be only spirit because the physical features that we have now will become utterly irrelevant.

EPILOGUE

Before closing, once again, I would like to give thanks to Jehovah, my Lord and Savior, for honoring me with the incalculable incomparably precious gift of using me as His servant and instrument to write this book. The purpose of this work is to share God's mystery with all men and women, without distinction, and to make it available to those who value and appreciate God's action to intensify the light of their understanding. Consequently, it will invigorate their desires to commit their lives to the kingdom of God.

For these reasons, I bless each, every one of you, in Jesus's name. As soon, as you finish reading this book, I invite you to join me in honoring Almighty God and to thank Him for revealing His mystery to us. At the same time, we can set the supreme, lifelong goal, faithfully and fully abiding by the two commandments that our Lord Jesus Christ left us. The first is to love the Lord our God with all our hearts, souls, minds, and strength. The second is to love our neighbors as ourselves.

As we take the first step of faith toward fulfilling both commitments to love in our hearts, it is the best time to ask God for help. These commitments represent a great qualitative and quantitative leap forward in our relationship with God, with our neighbors, and with the society in which we live. If we abide by these two commandments, we will see blessings overflow in our lives as never before. Amen.

Here is an interesting and astonishing note: Having finished writing this book and while still in the process of editorial review and final revisions, the Lord placed the title for the book in my heart—*The Mystery of God. Hidden Truths since Timeless Times.* So once again, I want to thank Jehovah, my Almighty God, because He has also confirmed that He is and has always been a just-in-time God. He is never late, even when we think He is taking too long. Praise the Lord!

TWO FINAL SUGGESTIONS

Whenever you find negative emotions and selfish thoughts appearing at the door of your heart, turn them away immediately, in the mighty name of Jesus, and paraphrase 2nd. Corinthians 10:5, making the following declaration:

> I take captive all my thoughts and feelings to make them obedient to Christ. Amen!

Now that you have reached the final reading of this book, and have a greater understanding of God's extraordinary purpose for your life. The way to reciprocate, honor and please Him is, on the one hand, confessing Jesus Christ as your Lord and Savior, becoming His son or daughter, and on the other hand, expressing your adherence and unconditional commitment to Him in the following way:

> Oh, Almighty God, my Lord, since I choose your word for my mouth, I choose your will for my life, and my trust rests on you. Amen!

Name: ______________________________________

Date: _______________________________________

BIBLIOGRAPHY

Charles, S. *Biblical Ethics and Social Change*. Michigan: Oxford University Press, 1982.

Cruz, C. *La Vaca/The Cow, Spanish Edition*. Florida: Taller del Éxito Publishing House. 2007.

DeVos, R. *Compassionate Capitalism: People Helping People Help Themselves*. New York: Plume Editorial. 1994.

Gladwell, M. *David and Goliath*. New York: Hachette Audio. 2007.

Gladwell, M. *The Tipping Point*. New York: Hachette Audio. 2007.

Lapin, D. *Thou Shall Prosper*. San Francisco, CA: Actionable Books. 2013.

Lee, W. *The Divine Economy*. Living Stream Ministry: Second Edition. 1986.

More, G. *Crossing the Chasm*. California: Harper Audio. 2012.

Munroe, M. *The Spirit of Leadership.* New Kensington, Pennsylvania: Whitaker House. 2007.

Munroe, M. *Becoming a Leader.* New Kensington, Pennsylvania: Whitaker House. 2008.

New International Version®, NIV®. Holy Bible. Copyright © 1973, 1978, 1984, 2011 by Biblica, Inc.™.

Scott, S. *The Richest Man Who Ever Lived: King Solomon's Secrets to Success, Wealth and Happiness.* Colorado: Water Brook Press. 2006.

ABOUT THE AUTHOR

Clinton Cruickshank is a believer, engineer, educator, politician, thinker, businessperson, and entrepreneur. He graduated from the University of Costa Rica (UCR) in 1973 with a bachelor of science in electrical engineering. He was a UCR professor from 1975 to 1976. He was head of the Electro-Mechanical Division of the Costa Rican Railroads between 1975 and 1985. He pursued studies in Railways Transportation at British Railways (BR) in 1977, 1978. Operations Manager (interim) of the Costa Rican Railways in 1982. Studied management with emphasis on transportation at British Transport Staff College (BTSC), England, in 1978. Became a member Congress between 1986 and 1990 and Vice President of the Congress in 1989.

Joined and became a member of the Full Gospel Business Men's Fellowship International (FGBMFI) in 1994. Baptized in 1997. Became member and later the President of the Union Church Association. Later he Joined Oasis de Esperanza's Church. He taught the Word of God, taking the Gospel of Jesus Christ to workers in his places of employment. Special guest to teach the Gospel at home groups, churches, and at the Full Gospel Business Men's Fellowship International (FGBMFI).

Founder, Director, and Instructor of the Caribbean Political Training School from 2011. Main Program: The 21st Century Political Leadership. Founder and Director of the Think-Tank: "The Circle of Reflection on Political Ideas" from 2013. Executive Director of the Innovative Ideas Commission of the National Liberation Party between 2013-2014. Presidential Candidate hopeful for the Costa Rican National Liberation Party in 2013. Training Director of the Center of Democratic Studies for Latin America

Awarded the Order of Alejo Zuluaga from the University of Carabobo, Venezuela, in 1989.

Invited as the main speaker at the gathering of experts, executives, and investors at Silicon Valley, San Jose, California, in 1989. Topic: "The Future of Telecommunications and the Possibility of Establishing a Silicon Valley in Costa Rica".

Head of the congressional visit to the People's Republic of China in 1989. A special guest speaker to the South-South Commission during the Tribute to Nelson Mandela in Caracas, Venezuela in 1989. Graduated with honors as M.B.A. at the University of Costa Rica (1996). Member of the Board of Directors of the Costa Rican of Railways between 2006 and 2014.

He has been a national and international speaker.

Author of several books, such as: *Un Gobierno Compartido: Para Ganar Bien y Gobernar Mejor* (*A Shared Government: To Win Well and Govern Better*). *El Método del Buen Gobierno: Un Camino de Éxito en el Arte de Gobernar* (*The Method of Good Governance: A Path to Success in the Art of Governing*), and *La Nueva Costa Rica: Hacia el Club Exclusivo de Países Ricos* (The New Costa Rica: Towards the Exclusive Club of Wealthy Nations), unpublished. He publishes articles on different topics of national and international interest.

Printed in the United States
by Baker & Taylor Publisher Services